BALATON

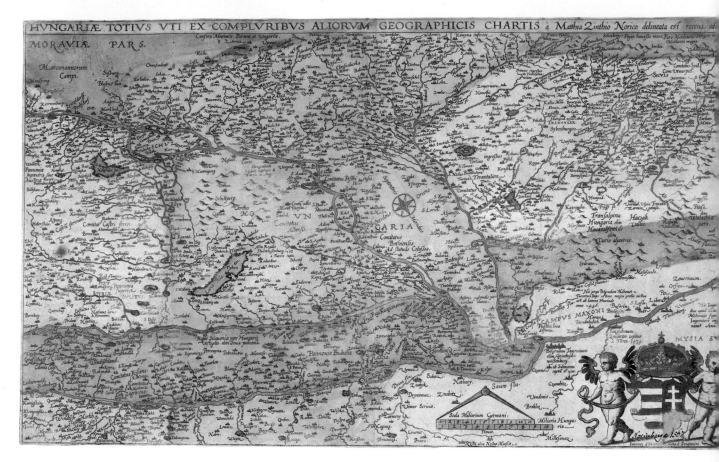

1. Hungary in 1567 (National Széchényi Library)

Fascinating traces of ancient cultures, earthworks, sepulchral mounds and other forms of burial, together with the diverse findings of archaeological excavations bear witness to how early on in history people discovered and appreciated this beautiful lake and its pleasant environs. In the first centuries after Christ the River Danube formed the *limes* or boundary of the Roman Empire in the Carpathian Basin. In the more protected interior of the fertile Pannonia province, in the Balaton area there were already agricultural communities around the *villae rusticae* or manors. Wine growing was already quite developed in this area, as around Aquincum, the town which subsequently became Budapest.

Illyrian and Celtic tribes composed the local indigenous population. However, the sons of many other peoples also settled in these parts. Having served in the Roman legions stationed here, they were granted land to start life afresh. Tradesmen from distant lands also settled in the province.

During the period of the Great Migration a permanent power centre emerged in the south-western corner of Lake Balaton to defend of the marshlands. Here we find a treasure trove of relics of mounted nomads of Turkic origin, Germans and Slavs. At the beginning of the 5th century Rome ceded Pannonia to Attila's people. It was at this time that the Eastern Goths, Theoderik the Great grew up along the shores of Lake Balaton.

In the 6th century the Longobards and Gepids fought over old Pannonia. The Longobards had been living in Pannonia since 546, but as early as Easter 568 moved south-west toward Italy, eventually founding Lombardy. The place of the Longobards was taken over by the nomadic Avars, who began to cultivate the land. Their rule was broken by the Franks of Charlemagne, but the people survived and were assimilated by the Magyars.

At one time this region formed a bridge between the separate northern and southern Slav areas. In 861 Father

Method of Slav-populated Mosaburg, one of the architects of the new Slavic writing and Cyrill's associate, paid a visit to the village of present-day *Zalavár*. The memory of the visit is preserved there by a fine statue.

The *Magyars* were of Eastern origin and had close ties of kinship with Turkic tribes, albeit speaking a Finno-Ugric language. They moved into the north and south of the Carpathian Basin in 896. In Pannonia, the region west of the Danube, the new Magyar domination grew along the Esztergom—Székesfehérvár—Tihany—Pécs axis, but it took the invaders several years to strengthen their grip.

Medieval kings founded monasteries around the Balaton and the Veszprém bishopric extended its rule to these parts. The royal estates in the Balaton area alternated with the huge lands of the noble families.

The area was populated by farmers, fishermen and artisans. Although the dreaded Mongol invasion did not reach this region, a major castle system was established here by royal decree as a safeguard against excepted attacks. Good examples are Tátika (1248—57), the castle of Sümeg (13th century), Tihany Castle, Csobánc (around 1255), and Szigliget (1260—62). These fortresses were blown up one after the other in later centuries to prevent them from falling into Turkish hands and were destroyed by the Turks themselves. Those that remained were destroyed on Emperor Leopold's orders in 1702, lest they should serve as a hiding places for rebellious magnates.

There was hardly any *social life* around Lake Balaton in the present sense of the word before the middle of the 19th century. In the Age of Reform, Balatonfüred became a centre of Hungarian intellectual life. Here the first Hungarian theatre was opened, men of letters gathered, and there was bustling social life in the town. A wealth of monuments from more recent times provide a historical background for the people who come for the water and sunshine on summer vacations.

2. View of Füred in the 19th century (Miklós Szerelmey, 1848)

3. Balaton landscape ▷

4. Tihany Peninsula

Lake Balaton is divided by the *Tihany Peninsula* into a wider north-eastern and a narrower south-western basin. The abbey towering over the peninsula shows the care the Church of the time took in choosing a site for its principal institutions. This building complex, visible from great distances, dominates the landscape, as though the eye of God protected the entire region from here.

This was not, however, the sole reason why we chose this place as the starting point for our tour. The Deed of Foundation of Tihany Abbey, drafted in 1055 by King Andrew of the House of Árpád and preserved at the Abbey of Pannonhalma, is a national relic. There are similar deeds of foundation dating from earlier times, however, it is in this Latin text the document that the first written Hungarian words appear — and not merely as placenames, but also in sentence fragments. Thus, this document is a linguistic treasure of the Finno-Ugric language family, as well as Hungarians. The present form of the *Abbey Church* is Baroque in style. The richly carved and gilded interior of the inner church is the work of the carpenter Sebestyén Stuhlhoff. The murals were painted by the great Hungarian masters of the 19th century, Bertalan Székely, Károly Lotz and others. In the original, 11th century croft of the church rests the founder, King Andrew, who died in internecine struggles. After the great vicissitudes of Hungarian history this is the only royal burial place that has remained on its original site and survived almost intact.

Today the Abbey houses the *Tihany Historical Museum*. Besides the exhibited objects, the fine Baroque architecture is noteworthy. In summer, musical performances are staged in the courtyard of the convent, with organ concerts inside the church.

Tihany also boasts of a string of other interesting sights, as the earthwork called *Old Castle* from the Early Iron Age. Others include the 11th century hermit caves carved into stone, which served as the cells of the Greek Orthodox monks who arrived with Andrew's wife, a native of Kiev. Special mention must be made of the fact that the whole peninsula is a *nature conservation area*. Always sparkling, the tiny and enchanting *Inner Lake* is an anglers' paradise. In the special relief of the peninsula, the geologist will immediately detect the hydroquarcite and spring limestone geyser cones. These were formed in the final phase of volcanic activity which shaped the structure of the entire northern shore of Lake Balaton. We can justly say that the fiery wines made from the grapes grown on this soil recall the old fires of the earth. It has been a long time since anyone saw geysers gush forth in this region, but many thermal springs feed the fountains and pools of spas.

At Tihany, the narrowest part of the lake a regular ferry service carries both pedestrians and motorists from spring through autumn. In fine weather, even this brief crossing can be a marvellous experience and many passanger regret when the ferry finally docks.

Club Tihany is an exclusive resort near the ferry crossing. This is the first hotel complex in Hungary — with 150 cosy bungalows besides the hotel — which offers not only meals, accommodation and entertainment, but organized recreation for its guests of any age in the family.

Tihany has character which is at once Mediterranean and Hungarian. This special atmosphere has been preserved despite the multitude of visitors each year. Tihany has its "clans"; year-round residents, people who have built summer homes here, and others who keep coming back year after year. They always find something new.

Finally, we must mention that local curiosity, *'goat's*

5. Tihany's Outer Lake (Külső-tó), a protected area

◁ 6. Baroque façade of Tihany Abbey Church
(1719—54)

7. The richly aborned church interior
(Sebestyén Stuhlhoff, 1753—65)

8—9. The relics of Balaton angling and the chimneyless "smokey kitchen" at the Open-Air Village Museum

nails'. These are fossil shells, washed out by the water from the sediments of the primeval sea. Legends, however, are far more captivating than fact. According to one, the ancient people of Tihany used to be rather aggressive folks, who rustled the goat herds of the neighbourhood. One day, however, a fierce storm swept all the stolen goats into the lake and their hooves, or 'nails' keep returning to the shove. Another version of the legend is about a golden-fleeced herd overpowered by a storm. Here, however, the cause is but a haughty princess who rejected the courting of the Lake Prince. The disappointed lad killed himself. Besides the losing her goats, the princess is in a cave. From this cave, she replies imprisoned to whoever addresses her, always shouting back what had been said to her. This takes us to the famous the *Tihany echo*. The echo may still be heard, despite various constructions projects, but not as well as before. By taking a little walk to the back of Tihany Abbey, you too, can test it.

From Tihany the road flanked by shady trees runs along the north-eastern shore of the peninsula to Balatonfüred. Before we reach this famous spa, we pass an industrial plant on the shore. The shipyards of Füred must be mentioned not only for the yachts it built. It was here that steam shipping started on the lake in 1846, turning the town into a major centre of Balaton shipping by the mid-19th century. The steamers Sümeg and Kisfaludy, the latter named after the poet of the Balaton region, started out on their journeys from here.

One of Füred's main attractions is the flourishing yachting scene. Each August the Füred Regatta, the great yacht race, offers an exciting day.

Füred's principal attraction is, of course, *bathing*. Strangely enough, bathing life in Balatonfüred had not included the lake for a long time. The people living around the lake fished in it, transported goods on it, drove their livestock there to drink, harvested reeds at the edge of the lake, and cut the ice in winter to fill ice-pits for the long summer. They did not, however, bathe in it — up to this century. The sour, carbonated thermal water of Balatonfüred did, however, acquire great fame at the beginning of the 19th century. The Füred tub bath was recommended for disorders of the heart and the coronary system, and its special drinking cure for stomach, bile and digestive pro-

10. Old building with the Abbey Church ▷

11. Surfing in Tihany Bay

blems. There is a hospital in Balatonfüred specializing in heart disorders. It has several hundred beds and today specializes mainly in rehabilitative treatment.

In 1926, the Indian poet Rabindranath Tagore, a Nobel Prize Laureate was a patient at the hospital. Like other famous guests of Füred, he planted a tree on the promenade. It is still there, amongst the trees commemorating other Nobel Prize Laureates.

The curative affect is enhanced by the geographical situation of the town. Füred, encircled by mountains, is protected from the North, but open to the South. Its microclimate is especially favourable. The town is also a favourite of those seeking culture and entertainment. In particular, it has a strong theatrical tradition, which has attracted a host of actors and writers. A good example is the great Hungar-

12. Club Tihany Hotel

ian story-teller, the novelist *Mór Jókai* (1825—1904), who to Hungarians is the embodiment of the tradition set by Victor Hugo and Jules Verne in France. Jókai owned two houses here, one of which he built together with his wife, the popular actress Róza Laborfalvi (1817—1886).

The many fine 18th and 19th century buildings which have been preserved or restored to their original beauty are constant reminders of Füred's flourishing past.

In 1825, guests invited to the *Horváth House* — built in Louis XVI style and still standing today — danced until dawn at the ball staged on the name-day of the beautiful girl to be "married off". That night, a handsome Hussar officer, Ernő Kiss asked in marriage the hand of Anna Horváth. They were shortly married. But the fate of the Hussar took a tragic turn. One of the heroes of the 1848—49 war of independence, he was among the thirteen Hungarian generals executed in Arad in the course of bloody retaliation.

Few remember this romantic and tragically ended marriage nowadays. But each year on 26th July, the *Anna Ball* is staged in Balatonfüred. In recent years the ball has become immensely popular with overseas expatriate Hun-

14—15. Club Tihany tennis court and swimming pool

13. Club Tihany mini-golf course

16. Beach of the Balatonfüred FICC Rally Camp Site

garians and their daughters. And since for a long time there had been no beauty peagants in Hungary, the Ball Queen elected here every year could, together with her two ladies-in-waiting, could be regarded as Miss Hungary and her runners-up. After dancing through the night, the three crowned beauties are drive around town in a coach for all to admire them. This is a splendid ending, a veritable festival for the people, after the spectacular ball of the night before.

17. Yacht harbour in Füred

18. Balaton anglers

Last but not least, it is worth visiting the *Lóczy Cave*, named after a great scholar of the geology of Lake Balaton and its environs. Lake Balaton is protected on the North, by the *Bakony Mountains*. However, often the wildest storms burst forth from here. For a long time the Bakony was the densest forest in the Carpathian Basin. It concealed castles and monasteries. Hunters roamed it. Swine herds were driven here from a far in winter-time to be fattened on the acorn. Those who knew only domestic-

19. The race is off…

20. The Neo-Classic Blaha Villa in Füred

22. The Neo-Classic Round Church (Kerek templom — 1841—46) of Balatonfüred

ated pigs would have considered them wild boars — hunter's prey rather than for slaughter by the butchers.

Besides the pusztas of the Great Plain, Bakony Forest was the main hiding place of the *outlaws*. Amongst them were popular heroes, the likes of Robin Hood, who only robbed the rich and helped the poor. The majority were, however, common criminals, often driven to crime by the miserable conditions of the times. Legend has it that the cellar of the *csarda inn of Nemesvámos* near Veszprém was designed to be so low in order that the nimble outlaws, armed only with sticks, pistols or light rifles similar to the Italian lupara, could escape through the back from the heavily armed gendermes.

Veszprém has been a royal free town for a thousand years, since the reign of Saint Stephen. It is an episcopal see, where before becoming archbishop of Esztergom, József Mindszenty was bishop. The traces of flourishing Baroque the finer sections of the Old Town of Veszprém preserve the atmosphere of the past. Here we find one of the most beautiful *episcopal palaces* in the country, the

21. The Jókai Mór Memorial Museum, Balatonfüred

work of Jakab Fellner (1765—76). Standing next to it is the 13th century *Gisela Chapel*, a significant historical monument from the Árpád period. The frescoes uncovered here, Byzantine in inspiration and depicting the apostles in life size, are the oldest in Hungary.

The Art Nouveau Petőfi Theatre was built in 1908 by István Medgyaszay. An interesting feature of this building is that the architect applied reinforced concrete for the first time in this country. The sgrafitto on the façade and the glass windows of the theatre are amongst the finest works of Hungarian Art Nouveau.

If you want to discover the heart of the Bakony, take an excursion to *Zirc* and visit the Abbey Church. The altar painting is by the 18th century Viennese master *F.A. Maulbertsch*, who did some of his best painting in Hungary. The library, a historical monument, as well the as museum, both named after the linguist Antal Reguly (1819—1858), who was born in Zirc, and the arboretum are well worth seeing.

Nearby *Csesznek Castle* and the sights along the road leading to it should not be missed, either.

Hungarian archaeologists have uncovered the remains of many Roman settlements around the lake. Of outstanding importance among these is the large, beautifully reconstructed *floor mosaic* unearthed at *Balácapuszta*, near Veszprém, and displayed in the hall of the Hungarian National Museum in Budapest. A huge mural depicting a sun-lit garden may be seen on the original site.

Between Veszprém and Tapolca, parallel with Lake Balaton, the stern Bakony range is separated from the

23. Balatonfüred's cardiatric hospital

24. *The Helka ship bar and café*

25. *The Anna Ball beauty queens*

26. *The Imre Kálmán Promenade*

27. *The bar of the Annabella Hotel*

gentler Balaton hills by the *Eger Waters* ten kilometers away. In its valley we find a string of old water mills mostly in the village of *Kapolcs* and its vicinity. Several of them are scheduled for restoration. The valley was protected by the Castle of *Nagyvázsony*, the property of Pál Kinizsi (?—1494). A miller's apprentice turned warrior, Pál Kinizsi was the commander-in-chief of King Matthias's (1443—1490) famous Black Army. Today, *equestrian games* are held outside his one-time castle in summer — with actors dressed in period costumes.

Fine china is produced in only a few places in the world. Located west of Veszprém, in the small community of Herend a porcelain factory founded in 1839 producess hand-painted china of artistic value. The visitor should not miss the factory's museum, which exhibits a full cross-section of Herend porcelain — traditional and new. The shop next to the museum sells the classic Herend china. Queen Victoria, the Barons Rotschild and others were among the early customers.

Badacsony produces rich, heavy wines, the most famous of the Balaton. The lighter, sprightly wines of Balatonfüred and *Csopak*, have a refreshing aroma. Although in both areas *Olaszrizling* is the main grape variety, the wines grown in Füred are softer, smooth and low in acid, whil those of Csopak have a more marked character. In the part of Csopak called *Stone Coffin Hill* not only Roman sarcophagi were found but also a Roman-age cellar and vessels for wine.

Most visitors to Füred, and the adjoining *Arács*, Csopak and *Kövesd* buy bottled wines, and like them. The lucky ones who get acquainted with a local grape grower, are taking to his cellar, wine house or home, to sample his own wines from the barrell. Wines — and not just wine. For the wine of not only each vintage, but the wine of almost every other barrel may be different in a good cellar, with a wide range of colour, taste and bouquet. And lovers of good wine agree that "there is pleasure in diversity".

In this area, the rock, or even the soil of the vineyards, is often reddish of even violet in colour. This is not the characteristic basalt of the Balaton hill country — which is grey — but a much older sand-stone stained to such an unusually lively colour by iron oxide.

28. The cosy cellar of the Hordó Csárda, Balatonfüred

Moving further East, we encounter much more that is worth seeing: a water-mill, old csarda-inns, well-preserved peasant houses and villas. A Neo-Gothic house in *Alsóörs* deserves special notice. Although this is a *Gothic mansion* from the 16th century, tradition has it that it was a tax-collecting house during the period of Turkish Ottoman rule. Today, the church, of Romanesque and Gothic origin but later modified in the Baroque style, belongs to the Calvinists. We can see traces of medieval painting on its exterior. The church of the nearby village of *Felsőörs*, formerly a *provost church*, is finer still. Built from reddishviolet local stone, the three-naved basilica towers over Mill Valley. The stone adornments on its façade and its columned gate preserve the atmosphere of medieval times. Its restoration twenty years ago earned wide international recognition among experts of historical monument protection. Next to it, the former provost building has been converted into an inn of an archaic-folkish character.

◁ *29. Row of cellars between Aszófő and Balatonfüred (1848—83)*

30. Typical red soil on the outskirts of Balatonfüred

31. Ruins of a medieval church, Balatonfüred

32. The church spire of one-time Alsódörgicse

33. The ruins of the church of Töttöskál (12th century)

34. Heart-shaped tombstones of the cemetery of Balatonudvari (19th century)

Near the neighbouring village of *Lovas*, archaeologists unearthed one of Europe's oldest mines. Thirty-five to forty thousand years ago, Stone Age man used tools made of bone to mine the local red clay, wich contained iron oxide. Mixed with grease, this red paint served for painting the body, to decorate both the living and the dead.

Moving along the shore of the lake, we will encounter a string of camping sites for motorists, and youths. At the peak of the holiday season, it is advisable to book in advance.

The entire northern coast of Lake *Balaton* is often compared to the Riviera, but perhaps this description best applies to the area near Balatonalmádi. On the shore that juts *Fűzfő Harbour* and the slopes rising above it, several old settlements merged to form a major resort. In *Vörösberény* the present *Calvinist church* is of medieval origin, albeit it has been rebuilt several times. The surriving

37. Village scene

40. Consecration of a bishop in front of Veszprém's episcopal palace (1765—76)

fortress wall built around it is a unique feature of the Balaton region. The community's *Baroque Catholic church*, the Parish Church of St. Ignotius of Loyola is also famous. It was built by the Jesuits of Győr at the end of the 18th century. It is still disputed who painted the beatiful frescoes inside but it is regarded as the work of the Viennese master Johann Cymbal. Standing next to it is a one-time Jesuit monastery in similarly Baroque style.

Balatonalmádi has a curious chapel of mixed age—a modern-age replica of a part of Buda's Sigismund Chapel. It was in this chapel section in Buda that the famous Saint Stephen reliquia, the Holy Dexter (the intact hand of the king) was once kept. This was eventually transferred to the *Saint Stephen Basilica in Budapest. Saint Stephen's*

41. Detail of the Trinity Statue (1750)

mosaic, salvaged from Sigismund Chapel, destroyed during the war, was taken to Balatonalmádi.

The lawyer and writer Károly Eötvös (1842—1916), whose book *Travel Around Lake Balaton* is an adventurous encyclopaedia of the landscape, also attaches a legend to Balatonalmádi. Once upon a time, when the counties enjoyed great independence, the *Torgyöpi Csarda (inn)* was built in Almádi in a way that the master beam of the bar was placed exactly over the borderline between two counties. One guest who ate or drank on one side of the table placed under the master beam, was in Zala County, while another enjoying a drink or two on the other side was sitting in Veszprém County. So what happened when the gendarmes pursuing the outlaws entered the premises? A glance at the uniform could tell which county sent them, and one needed only to jump to the other side

42. *View of Veszprém from the castle*

43. Zirc's Abbey Church with altar picture by F.A.Maulbertsch (1754)

44. The exterior of the church (1738—53)

of the table—to the other county. The gendarmes of the other county could not go over there...

Located in Almádi is the *Jancsi Kiss Villa*, of romantic fame. Jancsi Kiss was a handsome gipsy violinist, who enchanted an English countess with his virtuoso violin performance that she fell deeply in love with him. Indeed such romances were sparked off every now and then, but were usually casual affairs, the flame of passion soon extinguished. In this case, however, the romance turned out to be a lasting one, the countess taking the gipsy violinist as her husband. They lived in this villa for a long time. Even after the death of her husband the English lady stayed in Almádi, until the Second World War. Their children grew up in England.

45. The Zirc Arboretum

◁ *46. Kinizsi Castle, Nagyvázsony (15th century)*

48. The ruins of a Paulite monastery in Nagyvázsony

49. Stud in the Kerteskő landscape

In the gulf the road takes a big turn. At *Balatonfűzfő* the geological structure and landscape of the shore changes. On the eastern shore the water has washed out a high loess wall. The railway, the road, and, along the two, the narrow resort belt hardly fits between the reeds of the lake shore and the shaky loess wall.

From here the Balaton looks like a sea. Viewing it lengthwise, its water seems to disappear into infinity. The opposite shore is invisible. Fűzfő and *Balatonkenese* stretch towards each other, and would have merged but of the narrowing and sometimes marshy stretch of land between them.

Fűzfő is noted for the tiny well-preserved 13th century village church of *Máma*. Kenese's treasure is the extremely rare and beautiful Asian plant, the *"tátorján"* in the nature conservation area. This unique plant flowers in May. In hard times the poor ate its root.

The man-made caves of the Kenese high shore are called *Turkish* or *Tartar Holes*, because they were supposed to have served as a refuge at the time of the Mongol

47. Equestrian games in the courtyard of Nagyvázsony Castle

50. The ruins of Csesznek Castle (13th century)

invasion or the Ottoman occupation of Hungary. In reality, they were cave dwellings. People who could not afford even the cheapest housing sought shelter here.

There is a own nudist beach at Balatonberény. *Balaton-akarattya* is an inconspicuous bend of the 'Hungarian Sea' — excellently suited for nudism. The recently opened *Piroska Campsite* caters especially to that.

After Akarattya, along Road 71, we pass big orchards and vineyards before reaching the access to the M7 motorway. The holiday resort area changes into vast agricultural lands. Turning left here and driving across it, we would reach Budapest. However, our destination is the south shore.

The lake is the same but almost everything else changes. There are no hills over the shore , only the slopes of the gentle Somogy hills approach here and there. Passing through Balatonvilágos and Balatonszabadi-Sóstó

from *Balatonaliga* to Siófok, a strip of pine groves planted along the shore stretch at length. The old core of the villages is further away from the shore. The holiday resorts right up to the Szántód ferry crossing to Tihany, are growing into a single, ribbon-like settlement countinuing towards Boglárlelle. The narrow strips of open shore remaining between two communities have been made into beaches and campsites.

The village of *Balatonszabadi* lies away from the lake. *Balatonszabadi-Sóstó* or Salt Lake is a part of the village nearer to the lake. Like Tihany's Inner Lake, this shallow lake, was created by rain water. It is not suitable for bathing.

The town of *Siófok* is often referred to as the capital of the Balaton region. Its harbour is at the mouth of the *Sió Canal*. At the time of high water level, water is chanelled down to the Danube through the Sió. At the mouth of the

60. The 150 year-old Nemesvámos csarda-inn

canal a thick meshing prevents the escape of fish from the lake. The shipyards of Füred may only build ships of the size that can be sent down to the Danube through the Sió Canal. East of the Sió, past a wide beach, stretches the *Golden Shore* — lined by a string of hotels built on a strip of land reclaimed from the lake. Although almost the whole of Siófok serves the tourist industry, this is even more true for the vicinity of the Golden Shore, where numerous restaurants and snack-bars cater to the tourists in addition to the good hotels on the shore. West of Sió spreads the *Silver Shore*, which was also built on reclaimed land. Officially, this stretch already belongs to *Balatonszéplak*. There

61. The set table

◁◁ 55—59. The world-famous porcelain of Herend

62. *Peasant house in Füred*

is a row of trade union vacation homes but anyone may rent rooms not used by union members.

The Meteorological Observatory near the harbour handles the storm warning service from spring to autumn. The Balaton in fine weather is a peaceful lake—deceptively peaceful. Sudden summer storms can churn up its shallow waters to waves of extraordinary heights. The locals, familiar with the nature of the lake, notice the threat of darkening skies but the unsuspecting visitor should heed the warning of the yellow or red flares, and return to the shore immediately. Especially at risk are those venturing in on inflatable mattresses or in small boats.

63. *A Balaton wine grower*

◁ *71. Interior of the Provost Church (13th century) of Felsőörs*

72—74. The exterior of the church and details

◁ 75. *The ruins of the 12th century church of one-time Máma*

76. *The Vörösberény fortress church (13th century)*

77. *Yachts at Siófok*

A summer storm on Lake Balaton, which usually makes it way forcefully from the Bakony Mountains, is a spectacular sight and a memorable experience, viewed from the safety of the shore, of course...

Siófok has two museums. One, named after József Beszédes (1786—1852), an expert on water management, presents the natural life of the Balaton and the water management activities connected with it. The other museum commemorates *Imre Kálmán* (1882—1953), one of the last great masters of the Vienna—Budapest school of operetta. His works are still regularly performed both at home and abroad. And the Csardas Queen, the tune of which is known to millions, is a classic of the genre. The composer of the *Csardas Queen* was born in Siófok, and the Kálmán Imre Museum occupies two rooms of the house of his birth.

And last but not least, Siófok night life is the liveliest around Lake Balaton in the holiday season.

After Siófok we present two little villages on the southern shore, each made famous by a great painter. *Mihály Zichy* (1827—1906) was born in Zala in the manor standing in the middle of a very old park. Zichy was one of the greatest Hungarian masters, highly successful in Paris, and for decades the court painter of the Russian czar in St.

Petersburg. He was a master of virtuoso technique, who besides his grand historical works, earned international fame with his erotic sketches. The one-time manor now houses the Zichy Memorial Museum. The other small community, *Bábonymegyer*, was made famous by another painter, *Gyula Rudnay* (1878—1957), who lived and worked here. Rudnay was captivated by the Somogy landscape, with its gentle slopes and sun-kissed fields. In homage to his village, he painted frescoes for the local Calvinist Church.

The shallow and quickly-warming water of the southern shore of Lake Balaton make this area especially suited for families with young children. Also, the restorts on this side have a quieter atmosphere then, for example, Siófok.

Situated between Zamárdi and Balatonföldvár is the Szántód *ferry crossing*, together with its csárda, a Baroque historical monument. Here the Balaton is narrowest between the Tihany Peninsula, and the flat marsh land jutting into the lake at Szántód.

The full name of Szántód is *Szántódpuszta*. The word *puszta* often confuses many, even Hungarians. On the Great Plain it denotes extensive pastures with sparse vegetation (the *steppe* in geographical terminology). But the meaning of puszta is different in Transdanubia and

78. The beach of Siófok's Európa Hotel

84. *Szántódpuszta, detail*

85. *The opening of the equestrian days*

some other parts where it denotes something like a ranch, a complex of the manor and the homes of farmers and hired hands. The *puszta* were not village in their own right, but officially parts of the nearest community.

For a long time, the Benedictine monks of Tihany Abbey on the opposite side owned Szántódpuszta. In the 18th and 19th century they built the farm buildings that today house the *Manor Museum*. The Patkó Csárda was built by converting old servants' quarters into guest rooms. Its riding club serves the equestrian sports, which are now becoming increasingly popular around Balaton. Every year, at the end of July, Szántódpuszta hosts the St. Jacob's Day Festival and Fair. Today, the fair is less commercial and more of an entertainment but there is shopping as well.

Nearby *Balatonendréd* is famous for its fine *lace* like that of Brussels. The craft of making lace was introduced to this village, slightly away from the lake and therefore less affected by tourism.

At the Szántód ferry crossing one has to make a little detour from the main road. Taking Road 7, flanked by majestic trees, we reach the centre of *Balatonföldvár*. This place has a certain aura of elegance, in contrast with the more solemn atmosphere of the historical monuments on

86. *Riding school at Szántódpuszta*

the northern shore, or Siófok's striving for anything new. This settlement is at once traditional and modern.

The name Balatonföldvár comes from the *Celtic earthwork* dating from the Iron Age. Parts of it are still discernible on one of the peaks of the hills stretching near the shore of the lake. Földvár, unlike almost every summer resort along the Balaton, was not originally a farming or fishing village. At the end of the 19th century the land was still desolate and uninhabited. Other settlements, long inhabited, spread out and were transformed as summer bathing came into the vogue. Here a bathing resort sprung out of almost nowhere and grew into a community.

"The greatest Hungarian", Count István Széchenyi (1791—1860), played a key role in the creation of Balatonföldvár. The extremely rich Széchenyi family had large estates on the southern shore of Lake Balaton, and this particular stretch was theirs. Today, their villas still stand on the hill where the Celtic earthworks were.

Balatonföldvár did not develop spontaneously, but was built as a planned community by engineers. Perhaps this was why so many renowned engineers worked and settled here — amongst them Kálmán Kandó (1869—1931), whose inventions revolutionized the manufacturing of electric motors and the electrification of the railways.

88. Kőröshegy inn

89. The Piroska csarda-inn on Kőröshegy

87. Section of village courtyard

On the other hand, *Kőröshegy* which has already merged with Földvár, is historically one of the most interesting settlements in the southern shore. In the course of the restoration its *Gothic church*, which belonged to the Francescan monastery at one time, regained its original form and beauty. Its excellent accoustics contribute to the success of musical performances staged during the summer.

The story of the late-Baroque *Széchenyi Palace* is a romantic one. Count Zsigmond Széchenyi (1898—1967) was an impoverished landowner, but a splendid hunter. He spent his income, and later the earnings from his highly successful books and hunter's memoirs, on hunting expeditions to Africa, India and Alaska. In his one-time palace a small collection bears witness to the life and work of the great hunter and writer.

In contrast with aristocratic Földvár, *Balatonszárszó* is expressly middle-class in character. This small bathing resort is known to Hungarians mostly for its literary and political associations. It was here that one of the greatest Hungarian poets of the 20th century, Attila József (1905—1937) committed suicide by stepping in front of an approaching train. His memorial museum is in the house where he lived for a short time. During the war years, writers and intellectuals opposing the war and trying to find a way out for Hungary gathered at the so-called *Szárszó*

90. *Peasant-Baroque verandah of a residential*
◁ *building in Bálványos*

91. *Early 20th century gingerbread-marker's workshop in Zamárdi's folk centre*

conferences. These political meetings were disguised as ordinary summer gatherings of friends.

In *Balatonszemes*, which at one time used to be an important stage coach stop the Baroque-style stable of the old postal service has been converted into a small *postal museum*. In front of it stands a stage coach now out of service. The collection itself does not document the traditional post office, but the history and development of communication in general. A *Renaissance pastoforium* dating from 1517 is preserved in the chapel of the local Catholic church. The ancient settlement located here also used to be protected by an earthwork. Part of this has been washed away by the water of the lake. Later, during the Ottoman occupation a border fortress stood in this place — often exchanging hands. In 1900, however, there was an unexpected turn of events. A peculiar new castle named *Owl's Haunt* was built over the ruins of the so-called Fool's Castle. The plans were made by an Italian architect by the name of of Roman Marandini.

Travel books usually give *Balatonöszöd* only a brief mention. For several decades, most of this village was reserved as the exclusive use of communist party and government functionaries. The major changes that have taken place in Hungary over the past years will certainly affect this. Balatonöszöd is not the only Balaton resort that is bound to witness some major changes soon. Already several former communist party holiday homes have been converted into commercial hotels.

It may well happen that *Boglárlelle*, the name under which Balatonboglár and Balatonlelle merged in 1979, will separate under the new drive for local autonomy now spreading in Hungary. In contrast with Földvár's aristocratic and Szárszó's middle-class character, *Balatonlelle*, at least a certain part on the shore, reveals upper middle class traditions. There is, for example, a splendid three-story villa, once the property of a renowned surgean, surrounded by a huge park which was once an arboretum with separate gardener's quarters. There were many others like it in the same street, enclosed between the railway tracks and the shore. Most of these summer homes, which had their own stretch of beach, no longer exist. The land was needed for new buildings, roads, promenades and public beaches. On the other hand there is now a network of private pensions, cosy restaurants, cafés, wine bars and small shops. This can cater to far more visitors than ever before. Only the 'islands' now retain a trace of

⊲ *100. Harbour of the Balatonföldvár Yacht Club*

101. Surf and lights

exclusivity. Like most other summer resorts on the lake, Lelle, too, now caters to various demands — depending on the taste and wallet of the guests.

One of Lelle's buildings in a rural style houses a museum exhibiting the works of Antal Kapoli (1867—1957), perhaps the most famous of Hungarian wood-carvers, who was a herdsman. Besides his carvings which depict the life of the herdsman and outlaws — the main source of inspiration for folk artists — he also made portraits of historical figures. (His name refers, incidentally, to the community of Kapoly, near Siófok.)

A special feature of *Balatonboglár's* geography is that next to the loess hills of Somogy that stretch down as far as

102. Twighlight angling

◁◁ *103. The Baroque chapel of Kis-hegy, Balatonlelle*

◁ *104. Teleki's burial chapel (on 13th century foundations)*   *105. Roman tombstone at Balatonszemes*

the shore are the results of volcanic activity which created the range of mountains on the northern shore, albeit the hills are only of modest height.

In Boglár there is also a well-known state farm of orchards and vineyards which has its own wine cellars and *wine museum*. This state farm not only grows grapes for its own purposes, but also produces and markets grafts. It is worth looking for local wines not only on the northern but on the southern shore as well.

Boglár, too, has an earthwork, surrounded by a nature conservation park and a *spherical observation tower* brought here from the Budapest International Fair. It bears the name of János Xantus (1825—1894), who served as an officer in the 1848—49 Hungarian War of Independence. Later, in exile, he became an American marine captain, government official and diplomat. After his eventual return to Hungary he embarked on several journeys to South-East Asia. His collections laid formed the foundation of the Ethnographical Museum in Budapest.

On Chapel Hill next to Castle Hill there stand two cemetery chapels, one Lutheran, the other Catholic. In summer, art exhibitions are staged in the *"blue"* or *"red" chapel*, which no longer serve religious purposes. Theatrical performances and concerts are also held in these beautiful surroundings. Boglár's Chapel Hill is a centre for Hungarian avante-gard artistic exhibits — some of which have been kown to cause scandals but more of a political then an artistic nature.

Those fond of walking will enjoy climbing the gentle slopes that may be reached easily from Földvár and Boglárlelle. The look-out towers on these hills, especially Boglár's Xantus Look-out Tower, offer a breath-taking panorama of the opposite shore and the whole lake.

The nearby village of *Karád* is noted for a rare old type of *white embroidery*. The local folk art centre houses a collection of local folk dress and embroidery.

At *Fonyód* there are some real mountains. Like Boglár's "peaks", these, too, are of volcanic origin. At one time extensive marshland spread around the Sipos and Vár Mountain, only smaller parts of which have remained. The marsh protected the two mountains and prehistoric man on the island-like parts around them, the Romans who lived here, and later Fonyód's border fortress. For a long time this fort, built mostly with adobe walls, successfully resisted Turkish onslaught, eventually fell in 1575. (Along Lake Balaton only Tihany, sheltered by its peninsula,

106. *Ruins of the Castle in Kereki (13th century)*

107. *Church ruin in Rádpuszta (13th century)*

stayed on Hungarian hands throughout this period.) Situated above the castle area is the only folk monument of the area, the thatch-roofed *Press House*, with an adjoining wine cellar.

Fonyód comprises a string of bathing resorts along the shore, each with a name of its own. It was only later that the narrow populated strip on the shore, was built with meticulous planning. It caters mostly to holidaymakers and in winter life comes almost to a standstill.

Birdwatchers should note that Lake Balaton and its environs abound in various species. At the time of the great autumn—spring migrations the brilliant surface of water or ice serves as an important point of orientation, while the open waters are a place of rest for water fowl. In milder winters many birds arriving from the North stay here instead of proceeding further south. The remnants of the marshland around Fonyód the local fish ponds offer special delights to the avid bird-watcher. Well-equipped photographers can take some magnificent shots of such rare species as the *great or noble heron* of the *little heron*.

As at the beginning of the southern shore and at several places further along, the building of the holiday resort on the stretch of shore after Fonyód was accompanied by the planting of pine forests. The name *Balatonfenyves* („feny-ves" meaning pine forest) is indicative of this. Behind it spreads the partly drained marshland in which canals have been made. This area is called *Nagyberek*. Once the lake had a good-sized bay which was sealed off from the Balaton by the accumulated sediment.

The draining of Nagyberek was not quite successful. The water moving freely under the surface of marshland turned out to be too powerful. Consequently, unsuccessful and expensive farming was again replaced by extensive live-stock breeding, for example, of cattle raised in the open and never kept in stables. (This cattle is a cross of imported Texan and Hungarian breeds.) In season, many kinds of small and big game can be hunted here.

The *Balatonnagyberek* State Farm offers many facilities to visitors. There is a modern inn equipped with sauna, a riding school, a steeplechase course stud-farm, chuck-wagon riding, and so on. A brewery, naturally with a beer-house, has also been opened here by the Bavarian Hof-bräuhaus company.

Take the popular narrow-gauge railway to discover Nagyberek. Here are two suggestions for excursions. *Csisztapuszta* has excellent medicinal waters — brought to the surface by oil prospectors. Visitors have been flocking to its there pools for years.

108. The beach of the Boglárlelle campsite

Stretching over 1500 hectares, the *Fehérvíz Marshland* is a nature conservation area with a wealth of aquatic and bird life. You can visit it only with a guide, because moving about this marshland can be dangerous. But you can observe the wildlife of this area from a well-positioned lookout tower.

Proceeding toward Kaposvár, there is something to see in almost every village in the Somogy hill country. *Buzsák* is famous for its colourful *folk art* and *fairs, Lengyeltóti* for its arboretum, a holiday village is being built at *Rágnicapuszta*. In the nearby community of *Nikla* is the manor of *Dániel Berzsenyi*. He is regarded as the greatest poet of the Balaton region.

In *Somogyvár*, the ruins of the ancient Kupa or *Koppány Castle* are a reminder of Koppány, a tribal chief, who wanted to keep the Magyar religion and fought against King Stephen I, who had converted the nation to Christianity. Later, King Ladislas founded Benedictine abbey here with the help of Odilo, the abbot of St. Gilles. Outstanding amongst its recently unearthed buildings is the three-nave *basilica*. Indicative of the French spirit of the former abbey is a beautiful 11th century stone carving, which is displayed in the Hungarian National Museum.

110. *The Igal thermal baths*

111. *The interior pool of Zalakaros baths*

109. *Wine cellar in Igal*

113. *The Buzsák folk centre*

Balatonmáriafürdő, coming after Fenyves, is also a young community, around which vineyards have sprung up on the sandy soil. The *Saint Crucifix Parish Church* in *Balatonkeresztúr* has been built on medieval foundations and is adorned with murals of the *Dorfmeister School*.

The last settlement on the southern shore is *Balatonberény*. Situated directly opposite Badacsony, and boasting of one of the finest beaches, its appeal is enhanced further by the beautiful view. Its Baroque parish church preserves Gothic details. Next to it the folk centre of *Balatonszentgyörgy* houses items of folk pottery and Buzsák

◁ 112. *Folk dress*   114. *Merry-making at the fair*

115—117. Nature conservation area on the Little Balaton

folk art. Nearby *Csillagvár* was thought to be a border fortress that survived Ottoman rule in exceptionally good shape. In reality, an eccentric aristocrat of romantic sway, László Festetics built it at the beginning of the 19th century. Subsequently, Festetics was placed under guardianship by his family for his extravagant lifestyle. Today, the Csillagvár houses a museum and small restaurant.

We have now almost reached the mouth of the most important water source of Lake Balaton, the *River Zala*. On the two sides of the river spreads a huge delta, the *Little Balaton*, a spread of marsh that gradually separated from the lake. Several attempts were made to control it with canals, but it was found that this would ruin the whole lake. Today the marsh is restored to its original state so that its reeds may filter the river water and thus reduce the sedimentation of the Balaton and keep its water clean. The unique birds of this *nature conservation area* are no longer at risk.

The tiny community of *Vörs* stands on the edge of Little Balaton. So-called *tub boats* used to be made here, carved from a single tree, clumsy in shape, but safe. The folk centre of Vörs presents the wildlife and fisherman's life of the Little Balaton. Its Firemen's Museum exhibits material depicting the work and equipment of the rural volunteer fireman. The last bull herd is kept on *Kápolna Puszta*. The excellent spa of *Zalakaros* offers more than a medical cure — there is also a wealth of entertainment, recreational opportunities abound (angling, riding, hiking), and wine.

Opposite Vörs, *Zalavár* was a major centre around the middle of the 9th century, protecting the Balaton marshes. This area was owned by Ludwig of Bavaria who have it to the Slav leader Pribina as a fief. Excavations uncovered early wooden churches from the time of the Slavs' conversion to Christianity, by missionaries from Salzburg. In some places the stumps of pile and log roads more than a thousand years old can still be seen. They provided the only possible way to cross the marshland safely. King Stephen founded a Benedictine monastery at Zalavár in 1019.

Near the lake before Keszthely are Roman ruins at *Fenékpuszta*: an early-Christian *basilica*, the foundation walls of warehouses, and fortress walls. The Roman *cas-

118. *Bulls' herd at Kápolnapuszta*

119. *The River Zala at the Little Balaton* ▷

trum once guarded an important crossing stage here. Curiously, next to the Roman walls stand the luxory stables of the Festetics Stud farm, built in the Neo-Classic style. The feed-boxes were carved from red marble.

The inhabitants of *Keszthely* regard their city as the capital of Lake Balaton and not without reason. The Festetics family of counts and princes with ties of kinship to the English royalty were patrons of literature and science. On the other hand, some of the Festeticses were eccentrics, haughty aristocrats who refused to have anything to do with anyone but their own kind. Legend has it that one of them had separate roads built for himself in order not to have to return the greetings of anybody while out horse-riding or enjoying a coach drive.

From the middle of the 18th to the end of the 19th century, the *Festetics Palace* gradually gained its present form. Restored with years of dedicated work, it is now embellished with several groups of statues. With a total of 110 rooms, it is the third largest stately house in Hungary today. The huge ornamental garden is in itself an impressive

120—121. *View and bathing island of Keszthely's Helikon Hotel*

spectacle. The palace houses the *Helikon Museum*, named after the Helicon festivities staged by Count György Festetics at the beginning of the 19th century; they were noted for their poetic contests and attended by artists, scholars and aristocrats.

The principal treasure of the palace is the *library*, preserved intact, the first of its kind in the country. Credit for this must go to the collecting zeal of the erudite members of the founding family, their wealth from vast estates which ran to several hundred hectares. The reading room of the library is in the Empire style. The oak carpentry is the work of a local master. In most of the palace rooms we can see elegant furniture, interior decoration and ornamental objects, as well as family and other paintings. Hunting and equestrian sports in the Balaton region are also depicted here. The arrangement of the material is not very mu-

seum-like, but meant to give an idea of the life of the old aristocracy. Recently, a permanent exhibition of one of Europe's biggest *weapon collection* has been opened here.

Leaving the palace and walking towards the lake on the main street we can see buildings in the Neo-Classic, Louis XVI, eclectic and the Romantic style. Some of the small shops in these houses have preserved their old form and furnishings. In this inner part of Keszthely, the charm of olden times blends harmoniously with the bustle of the crowded bathing resort and regional centre. In Kossuth Street stands the house where *Károly Goldmark* (1830—1915), composer, of the opera Queen of Sheba, was born.

In the *Gothic church* in the town's main square 14th and 15th century murals have been brought to light from under the plaster-work. Now restored, these are considered by art historians to be extremely valuable. A garden of ruins stands by the church.

In nearby Georgikon Street a plaque commemorates the *school of agriculture* founded by György Festetics — the first of its kind in the world. In Bercsényi Street is a row of of farm buildings, now housing the *Georgikon Manor Museum*.

Although the old collection of the *Balaton Museum* was destroyed during the war, it has since accumulated considerable material. Facing Keszthely Bay, the huge *Helikon Park* is a gallery of statues.

At *Hévíz*, the lake's natural water attracts visitors to this famous *spa*. You can take a swim from the wooden bath houses on the shore. The lake is surrounded by sanatoriums and health resort hotels. One of the best, the *Hotel Aqua* has 35 rooms designed especially for the disabled. To lift the spirit there is a variety of entertainment, including one of the few recently opened *gambling casinos*.

The Indian water-lily is a sensitive of even the smallest changes in water temperature and the micro-climate of the lake. Recently, nearby bauxite mines, which posed a potential threat to the water supply, were closed down in order to save the lake and its medicinal water. Skin divers have discovered that in the cave underneath the lake the karst-water and hot volcanic springs flow into each other.

The community of *Egregy*, which belongs to Hévíz, can be reached with a little detour. Its 13th century church is

122. *View of the Festetics Palace (18th—19th century), Keszthely*

123—124. *The façade of the palace and its embellished Neo-Baroque gate (19th century)*

one of the finest and most valuable *historical monuments from the Árpád period.* Its old walls and stone steeple dominate the landscape.

Reaching *Rezi Castle* on our way to Sümeg, we will discover a cave on one side. This too, was at one time brought into being by a thermal-water spring. The several hundred years old *Gyögyös Csarda-inn* makes for a good rest on the way. Legends about long-gone outlaws are still alive here, and the *graves* of two popular bandits never lack flowers.

The town centre of *Sümeg* is full of well-preserved old buildings. This small town used to be the favourite summer haunt of the bishops of Veszprém, who were attracted by the good Sümeg wine. Their love of pomp and luxurious buildings enriched Sümeg's townscape. The colourful *Maulbertsch murals* depicting the life of Jesus in the local parish church are some of the master's finest works. The church is often referred to as the Sistine Chapel of Central Eastern Europe. The 31-room bishop's palace of Sümeg is a Baroque masterpiece from the 17th century.

Standing nearby is the birthplace of the Hungarian poet *Sándor Kisfaludy* (1772—1844). Kisfaludy fought in the Napoleonic Wars and spent years in French captivity. The memorial museum in the house where he was born mirrors the life of the gentry of the times, as did the Festetics Palace of Keszthely the life of the aristocracy.

On a steep mountain above the town stands *Sümeg Castle*. This huge Gothic fortress is an exciting sight from far and near, impressive even in its ruins. Interestingly, a private entrepreneur has taken over the maintenance and operation of the castle, taking some of the load of historical monument protection off the state. This is an unusual and still untested arrangement in Hungary but if it proves itself foreign investors may possibly join.

East of Keszthely, below the Keszthely Mountains, we reach a stretch of the lake entirely different from anything we have seen so far. Under the sun-warmed southern slopes traditional peasant life has survived for a long time. Twenty years ago splendid small vineyards and romantic press houses were still offered at very low price. Few holidaymakers came here, to *Gyenesdiás* and vicinity, the last places where the summer home building boom arrived.

Above the holiday resort, the hills, partly cultivated, partly forested, offer excellent views of the landscape, stamped by the signs of winegrowing. Roman historical

125. *The great hall of the Helikon Museum library, with its original interior*

monuments bear witness to continuous habitation since the Age of the Antiquity.

Froming a part of *Vonyarcvashegy* and almost jutting into the Balaton is *Saint Michael's Hill*, previously an island with a chapel and cemetery. The dead were taken here by boat. The wine house once belonged to the cellars of the Festetics estate.

For those who wish to spend time away from the beaches, we especially recommend a stay in *Balatongyörök*. The extensive woodland situated above this community is accessible by with a wide network of footpaths for hikers. Detailed guidebooks furnish information on numerous points of interest, rocks and look-out towers worth visiting. The *Szépkilátó ("Fine View")* look-out tower is the best-known of its kind in the whole Balaton region. There is a beautiful panorama of Badacsony from here. The

126—128. The ornamental stairway and music hall of the palace and a panelled room

shady pine trees were planted by Mary Hamilton, related to the English royal family, the wife of Prince Tasziló Festetics.

The coastline turns north-east at Györök. At this point Road 84, the shortest route across Transdanubia from the direction of Sopron and Vienna, reaches the lake.

In the bay of the Tapolca Basin, at *Balatonederics* we encounter *mementoes of Africa*. It was here that Endre Nagy settled after returning to Hungary. He had lived in Tanzania for several decades — organizing hunting expeditions, as well as laying down the foundations of modern game protection and management. He introduced in Africa the "hunting industry" and game protection established in Hungary. He brought to Lake Balaton his ethnographical collection and trophies.

The *Tapolca Basin* was once a bay. Rising out in the

130. Keszthely's Gothic church (14th century, with 19th century spire)

middle is *Szentgyörgy Hill*, a good-sized basalt volcano. Its core, exposed by stone quarries, could illustrate geological lectures. Valuable vineyards cover the slopes. Szentgyörgy wine is "the wine of wedding nights". It is believed that it makes the woman yield and, more importantly, strengthens the man.

Perhaps this is why the *Tarányi Press House*, one of the finest folk historical monuments of the Balaton hill country, stands here. It was built towards the end of the 18th century in a slightly provincial Baroque style. This well-kept building today houses a tavern, with a spectacular view of the lake.

Tapolca itself is situated further in. The fate of its *grotto*, an underground lake once approached by boat, is threatened by the nearby bauxite mines. Formerly a quiet and small town, Tapolca has been both positively and adversely affected by the mining industry. On the outskirts the mining company built huge Y-shaped houses of almost sky-scraper proportions.

The three mounds of *Szigliget* are not extinct volcanoes, but are nonetheless volcanic, made up not of hard basalt, but of softer tufa. For this reason, fortunately, mining has not harmed it. We should note the old ferry wharf, the fine streets and ancient houses of the fishing village, as well as the ruins of the *castle* which fulfilled important military purposes for centuries. The former Esterházy Palace and arboretum park serve as a place of rest and work for writers and artists. The whole area is part of the *Badacsony Landscape Conservation District* in which special care is taken to preserve the geological assets, landscape, historical monuments and folk art of Badacsony and its environment.

Szigliget is a real gem. Its atmosphere, as well as the multitude of visitors frequenting it, is comparable to Ti-

131. The Romanesque building of Egregy cemetery chapel, Hévíz

132. Lake Hévíz, with bathing houses ▷ erected over the water

hany. It is, however, cosier because here the holiday resort and the old village are not so distinctly separated. Historical monuments include a castle, an old church and the ruins of an earlier church built in the old village, which has an intact spire. Of its more recent buildings, a row of peasant homes have been placed under protection. The local people here take special care to restore their homes in style. Modernizing is usually confined to the interior.

The name *Badacsony* refers to both the long, coffin-shaped mountain and the five communities nestling around it: Lábdihegy, Badacsony, Tomaj, Tördemic and, hiding under Ábrahám Mountain, Örs. Basalt, valuable for road paving, was quarried here for a long time, now banned — the first real victory of the Hungarian Greens, nature conservationists and environmentalists. The famous "basalt organs" were created when volcanic lava gradually cooled and the molten matter solidified in the form of regular hexagonal coloumns. These were mutilated by mining.

Besides the micro-climate — harsh winter, many chilly nights, hot summer, long, sunny autumn — the secret of the inimitable character of *Badacsony wines* lies in the soil. After the world-famous wines of Tokay, Badacsony and Szentgyörgy produce the best in the Charpathian Ba-

sin. Do not look for red or light wine here. The pride of Badaacsony is heavy, may be dry but more often slightly sweet. Its colour is crystal clear, the bouquet discrete, but nonetheless full of character. Instead of reading, you should taste it. But be careful when sampling. Badacsony wine can be deceptive. It usually feels weaker than it actually is, and reveals its true strength only after a time — mostly when we have left the cellar and returned to the fresh air.

Badacsony, which is now merged with Tomaj, is a memorial place for literature. Early in the 19th century it was a centre of fledgling Hungarian lyrical poetry. The poet Sándor Kisfaludy owned a vineyard in these parts and this poems are attached to the landscape. His own romantic love story, too, is connected with Badacsony, where he met the beautiful Róza Szegedy who became his wife at a Badacsony grape harvest. Their memory is preserved by their house, now the *Szegedy Róza Museum of Literature*, and by the *Kisfaludy House*, their former press house, now a popular wine bar. Mention must go to yet another Badacsony museum — the *Wine Museum*. It exhibit the relics of wine growing, but the visitor will find numerous establishments in the vicinity where he can actually taste the wines of Badacsony.

The painter *József Egry* (1883—1951) devoted his

133. Aqua Beach of the Thermal Hotel, Hévíz

whole life to Lake Balaton. His memorial museum is well-known to regular visitors. A master of plein-air, Egry was captivated by the changing lights of the water surface.

From the *Kisfaludy Look-Out Tower*, but also from other points, there are magnificent views of the lake, the lights and shades of colour that had enchanted József Egry. Footpaths on all sides lead to the mountain peak and the basalt organs. They say that once these organs did, in fact play music. After a rainfall, the warming and expanding tone makes a crackling sound. A longer hike will take us to a smaller and concealed volcanic peak, *Gulács*, above *Nemesgulács*. The *Folly Arboretum* rich in pine species, is a good look-out spot over *Badacsonyőrs*.

Making a detour from *Ábrahámhegy* towards Salföld, there is an abandoned mill in the valley. Near *Salföld*, we can see the finely restored ruins of a Paulite monastery built in the 13th century. *Kékkút* is famous for its "acid water" and mineral water springs. The water is bottled for export overseas. A Roman altar stone devoted to nymphs has been uncovered near the spring. An ancient Christian basilica is another reminder of the age and significance of this settlement. Kékkút is already halfway along the road to the Castle of *Csobánc*, above *Gyulakeszi*, perhaps the finest of the romantic castles of the Balaton hill region.

These castles, which have fallen to ruin, are the popular theme of romanticism. No wonder that Sándor Kisfaludy preserved the legends and miths surrounding them — singing of the idyllic or tragic story of these castles, the chronicle of a love affair or bloody battle of bygone times.

It is worth making a brief detour to *Ecsér* and visit its protected garden of ruins and church. Similar care is being taken of the ruins of the Romanesque church of *Révfülöp*.

Situated above Révfülöp is the *Káli Basin*. We have already touched its edges when passing Salföld and Kékkút. At Kővágóőrs old peasant dwellings and the manors of the gentry farm a homogeneous village landscape. Nearby rise the huge rocks of the *Kőtenger* ("sea of stone" of which little is left. Legend has it that once as many as six couples could dance the csardas on the flat rocks.

The changing landscape, the many ruins, the valley between Tapolca and Veszprém, and the tiny villages offer countless sights of interest to the visitor. Today this region, too, is entering the mainstream of tourism. Small restaurants and wine bars have been opened, those who wish to avoid the crowds on the beach take the rooms let by the locals.

134. *Drink bar at the Park Hotel*

135. *Gambling galore in Casino Hévíz*

136. The 13th century ruins of Sümeg Castle

Arriving at *Balatonszepezd*, around the middle of the northern shore, we will come across a church of medieval origin with Romanesque and Gothic elements. A memorial stone carved with a peculiar wrinting deserves special mention. It is called *Pogánykő* and was erected by the ethnologist and historian Gyula Sebestyén (1864—1946) near his English-style villa. Sebestyén proved the authenticity of the "Magyar" runic writing of the pagan era, of which very little evidence has survived because it had been carved on wooden sticks or boards. Runic writing is of Turkic origin and character. In all probability, the Huns also

137. F.A. Maulbertsch: The Birth of Jesus (1757—58), detail from an altarpiece

138. The interior of Sümeg's parish church, ▷ with F.A. Maulbertsch's frescoes

139—140. Tapolca — the old water-mill of the Malomtó now houses Hotel Gabriella

used it. Among the Magyars, it was used longest by the Székelys of Transylvania. Even until recently a kind of runic writing was used by the herdsmen of the puszta.

Hills clad with pine woods, plateaus and large vineyards surround the village of *Zánka*. The church of the old village dates from the Roman era, but has marked Baroque features. The big *youth camp* on the side of Akali has been the summering place of thousands of Hungarian and foreign children for many decades. But designation "camp" can be misleading for a complex of many stone buildings, too much concrete and asphalt.

Half a dozen roads run together a Zánka. It is easy to reach from here the Káli Basin and every one of the small villages of the Balaton hill country lying east of it.

Located in these parts is *Óbudavár*, the smallest village of the Balaton region with a population of some 80 people.

It has been inhabited continuously since medieval times. Its old buildings are carefully preserved; in the early-19th-century wash house women did their washing standing in the fresh water of the spring.

We have almost completed our tour and approach Tihany. Five tiny villages once stood in the present site of *Dörgicse*. The ruins of three old churches can still be seen. Nobody knows why but two of these were built together with two naves and two chapels.

Above *Balatonakali*, now merged with Dörgicse, we encounter a group of 19th-century two-story press houses on the slopes of *Fenye Hill*. We can find similar press and wine houses in many places along the northern shore. Most of them also offer a good view, either of the lake, or of a small valley or basin embraced by the wine-growing hills and slopes above the lake.

141. The peasant-Baroque Tarányi press house (18th century), and the Lengyel Chapel on Szentgyörgy Hill

The *press house* is part of the vineyard, used for longer stays only occasionally, mainly at the time of the grape harvest. The *wine house* of similar use has a cellar attached to it. The two designations are usually interchanged, the difference blurred by current language usage. Tourist maps indicate press and wine houses with tiny dot-like squares on the hill slopes. It is worth looking for these when taking a walk. Most wine growers are proud of their wine and often invite the visitor for glass or two. This is, of course, a more memorable experience than visiting the roadside csarda for a taste of the local wine. Should you wish to buy, the wine of the growers is usually better and cheaper than what is bottled by big companies.

At *Balatonudvari*, in the protected cemetery alongside the road, we encounter some fifty *heart-shaped tomb-stones* dating from the first half of the 19th century. Who carved them, who brought this shape of tombstone into the vogue? Nobody knows. Similar stones can also be found elsewhere, but not in such large number.

The village of *Örvényes* has a several hundred years old water-mill. Its important feature is that it functions. It mills very fine flour, the kind used to make *rétes*, or strudel, one of the tastiest Hungarian pastries. Strudel dough is kneaded, then stretched extremely thin to make fine, crisp layers. Real strudel dough, that is thin enough to be transparent, can be made only of wheat with high gluten content. It is filled with many different kinds of filling, sweet or savoury. Most common are the apple, sour-cherry, cottage cheese and cabbage strudel.

Before turning back to Tihany, we note the cellars of

142. Badacsony view from the ruins of Szigliget Castle (13th century)

Aszófő in the mouth of the valley. These mostly date from the second half of the 19th century and are of a late-Baroque character. Excavations at the church of the former village of Kövesd nearby, substantiated the legend that the inhabitants of the village sought refuge from the Turks in the church, which was then set on fire by the soldiers. Now in ruins, the church of Kövesd was built over Roman foundations.

We have now come a full circle — from Tihany to Tihany. Let us now take a brief journey in time, through the year.

Few people think of visiting Lake Balaton in the autumn, even though this part of the year is usually warm and sun-

143. Gate of nobleman's manor with coat-of-arms (17th century), Szigliget

145. Grapes

146—147. Old cellar and press house next to the ▷
Balaton

◁ **144. View of Badacsony from the wine hill of Györök**

ny here. The landscape is exceptionally enchanting and this is also the time of the grape harvest with its host of colourful folk customs and traditions.

In the spring almond trees burst with lilac petals, the peach trees are covered in light-pink, and the flowering cherry and sour cherry dress the landscape in brilliant white.

Winter can also be a great experience. Those who have seen Lake Balaton in wintertime, with the entire surface frozen, will invariably return year after year. In most years the shallow lake freezes at the end of December or early January. Windy weather after the onset of cold days will make the surface of the ice wavy with thousands of tracks. When there is no wind, howewer, the ice surface will be perfectly smooth, ideal for skating. In addition to *skating, ice-sledding* and *ice-yachting* are most popular. The passenger propels the ice-sled slowly with two sticks, but powerful winds push the ice-yachts to high speeds. This sport therefore calls for expertise.

Only parts of the lake are suitable for these sports, even when not covered by snow. Those sojourning around the lake in winter may be awakened in the middle of the night by loud bangs, the noise made by the ice breaking up.

When the weather becomes milder the ice expands and tablets of it pile over each other to form shaky bridges. When moving water reappears, the piles of ice collapse and some tablets are washed on to the shore. If the temperature drops below freezing and a strong wind whips up the still unfrozen water, the spray freezes in a thick layer of ice and brilliant icicles on the reeds and the trees on the shore. The spectacle is breath-taking, especially when the sun comes out.

Few hotels are open along Lake Balaton in wintertime because they cannot be heated. It is not difficult though to find accommodation. The beauties of winter on the lake, the special mood out of the tourist season make spending some time here a good choice.

We should not forget that the medicinal baths are operating all the year round. And the same holds for the famous wines of the Balaton. Throughout the year the wines grown on the volcanoes and red sand stone are just as fiery and irresistible — as the summer sun. Quite naturally, off season it is perhaps even easier to get close to local people, make friends and enjoy their traditional hospitality.

151—153. Grape harvest feast

154. Lake Balaton in winter ▷

LAKE BALATON

With its water surface covering almost 600 sq. km, Balaton is the largest lake in Central or Western Europe. It is 75 km long and its width varies between 5 and 12.5 km, at the Tihany Strait the width narrows to only 1.5 km. The lake's average depth is 3 metres, it deepest at Tihany, 11 m. Although there had been a sea where now Lake Balaton lies, the lake is not the remnant of the sea. It is relatively young, several 10 thousand years old. A geological sinking became filled up with rainwater.

The lake has the clearest water in Europe and needs protection from the harmful effects of modern life. Motorboating is not allowed here, thus hundreds of sailboats, thousands of windsurfers and bathers enjoy a quiet holiday here.

The water is often referred to as silky, which is not merely a poetic epithet. It is slightly alkaline, soft and, because of the fine floating mineral components, the water actually is a thin effervescent water. Sun therapy, the microclimate and the water which, though not salty but rich in minerals make bathing similar to that on the seashore, from May till early October.

Lake Balaton is not a gigantic swimming pool only but real living water. Fish are caught by fishermen in smaller or larger boats and by patiently waiting anglers alike. Fish supply is helped by artificial breeding as well.

As for fish dishes now, the two favourite local fishes are the modest bream (Abramis brama), a cheap kind belonging to the carp family. Smaller pieces are fried in oil or fat and eaten together with the crispy bones. The other variety is the pike-perch (Lucioperca lucioperca), one of the tastiest foods in the world. It may grow to a weight of 10 kgs, the smaller ones are called pike and the bigger pikeperch. They are fried in one too, but while bream are sold in small bistros along the shore, pike-perch is a luxury offered in elegant restaurants.

Although Hungary's climate is mostly continental, in the south of the country and around Lake Balaton mediterranean effects are stronger. Thus the climate is very pleasant, and especially on the southern slopes of the northern shore there grow many mediterranean plants such as almond trees, figs and pomegranates too.

The number of permanent inhabitants in the region has grown in two decades from 100 thousand to 150 thousand, but in the summertime this figure doubles. Part of the shops and restaurants are thus open in the summer only.

The railway runs right along the southern shore, in the north it makes a turn around Badacsony Hill. The whole area has a well developed autobus network. By car Balaton is of an access from Budapest on highway M7. Coming from Vienna though, if motorists cut down via Sopron-Sárvár or take highway 84 or 83 at Győr towards Pápa and Veszprém, they can spare time and gasoline and also it is more probable that they will see beautiful sights, quaint old towns and villages, historic monuments, small restaurants or apartment houses.

SIGHTS TO SEE

In Hungary, museums, memorial houses, historical monuments, etc., are usually open to the public between 10 a.m. and 6 p.m. from Tuesday through Sunday. They may also be visited on Church and public holidays, but are closed the following day. They are also closed to visitors on 1st January, 26th December, and Easter Monday.

In our directory the name of the builder-embellisher of the historical monuments is in parentheses, and the date of completion or major reconstruction is also indicated.

SOUTHERN SHORE

SIÓFOK
- József Beszédes Museum of Water Management, 2 Sió utca
- Imre Kálmán Memorial Museum, 5 Imre Kálmán sétány
- Wine Bar (cellar and yard building), late 18th c. Baroque, 43 Fő utca
- The minerals of the Carpathian Basin (private collection), 10 Kálmán Imre sétány
- Museum of Radio Communication, 2 Erdei Ferenc utca

ZAMÁRDI
- Roman Catholic Church, Baroque (1774), with Baroque interior, Fő utca
- Zamárdi folk centre (peasant dwelling, 1847), 83 Fő utca

SZÁNTÓDPUSZTA
- Exhibition Place for Szántódpuszta landscape history, Manor Museum, one-time manor building complex, with the relics of 18th–19th century farming. Annual St. Jacob's Day fête and lace fair at Balatonendréd
- Christopher's Chapel, Baroque (1735)

SZÁNTÓDRÉV
- Ferry Csárda-Inn (cart-shed, 18th c.)

KŐRÖSHEGY
- Roman Catholic Church, Gothic (14th–15th c.), converted several times, Petőfi Sándor utca
- Former Széchenyi Palace, late Baroque (c. 1790), in it the Africa hunter Count Zsigmond Széchenyi's memorial exhibition, 71 Kossuth utca

BALATONSZÁRSZÓ
- Attila József Memorial Museum, 7 József Attila utca

BALATONFÖLDVÁR
- Exhibition of Development Plans for Lake Balaton, 51 József Attila utca

BALATONSZEMES
- Post Office Museum, one-time manor stable, Baroque (mid-18th c.), 46 Bajcsy-Zsilinszky utca
- Hunyady Palace, Baroque (18th c., converted), 2 Gárdonyi Géza utca
- Granary, Baroque (18th c.), 4 Bajcsy-Zsilinszky utca
- Roman Catholic Church, Gothic (14th c., converted c. 1742), Fő utca
- Owl's Haunt, Neo-Romantic building (20th c.), Bagolyvár utca

BOGLÁRLELLE
- Antal Kapoli Memorial House, 35 Kossuth utca
- Locksmith's workshop, one-time iron-smith's workshop, folkish character, 52 Szabadság utca
- Former Jankovich Manor, Baroque (1712), 1–3 Petőfi utca
- Roman Catholic chapel, Baroque (18th c.), late Baroque furnishings, Kishegy
- Rodin: The statue of a woman stepping into the water (replica), next to the pharmacy
- Former Bárány Manor, Neo-Classic (1835), converted, 14 Szabadság utca
- Balaton Museum Ship (in service between 1870–1875), in the harbour
- Lake-side Gallery, Napospart út
- Blue Chapel, Lutheran (1856), on Chapel Hill
- Roman Catholic Red Chapel (1892), Chapel Hill
- János Xantus spherical look-out tower

FONYÓD
- Ruins of Lower Castle and fort church, with fort and earthwork system (12th–14th c.), 3 Kupavár utca
- One-time press house, now a fisherman's csárda-inn and wine bar (mid-19th c.), 17 Lenke u.
- Huszka Villa. The famous operetta composer's summer home (20th c.), Villa-sor, Bélatelep
- Harbour (1906) and pier (1897)
- Look-out tower on Sípos Hill (207 m)
- Fehérvíz Primeval Marshland. Nature Conservation Area, Balatonfenyves
- Summer Gallery, Fürdő utca

BALATONKERESZTÚR
- Roman Catholic Church, Baroque on medieval founda-

tions. (Design by Kristóf Hofstadter, 1753–1758). Murals inside, Dorfmeister School, c. 1760. Rococo furnishings (c. 1757), 5 Ady Endre utca
— Former Festetics Manor, Baroque (mid-18th c.), Ady Endre utca
— Granary, Baroque (18th c.), 19 Új Élet utca

BALATONBERÉNY
— Roman Catholic Parish Church, Gothic (15th c., converted into Baroque). Steeple from 1800, 90 Kossuth utca
— St. Wendelin's statue, Baroque (1793), 58 Kossuth utca

BALATONSZENTGYÖRGY
— Star Castle, early-Romantic (1820–1823), Irtási dűlő
— Folk Art Centre, originally a pedestalled house with a chimneyless kitchen. (1836), 68 Csillagvár utca
— Trinity Statue (18th c.), 40 Csillagvár utca
— Statue of St. George. The figure itself is late Baroque (c. 1800)

THE ENVIRONS OF THE SOUTHERN SHORE

ÁDÁND
— Former Csapody-Palace (18th c.), converted, today houses Agricultural Vocational School, including the Specialist Collection of the History of Agricultural Technology, 4 Árpád utca
— Roman Catholic Church, Baroque (1747). The entire furnishing is Baroque, Árpád utca
— St. John of Nepomuk (1813) and Immaculata statue (1816), late Baroque, Church Garden, 8 Árpád utca
— Church ruin, Romanesque style with Gothic addition. Hetye

SÁGVÁR
— Roman Catholic Church, baroque (1756), Baroque furnishings. Petőfi utca
— Statue of St. John of Nepomuk, Neo-Classic (1830). Petőfi utca
— Roman camp (Tricciana castrum), walls (3rd c.)

ZALA
— Zichy Manor, Romantic (18th c. origin, converted in the 19th c.). Protected park. Today the palace houses the Mihály Zichy Memorial Museum. Its collection includes the painter's works and his Caucasan ethnographical and applied art collection, 20 Zichy Mihály utca

BÁBONYMEGYER
— Lutheran church, Neo-Classic (1840). Neo-Classic furnishings. Altar pictures by Gyula Rudnay (1878–1957): The Three Magi. Bábony, Petőfi utca
— The statue of the painter Gyula Rudnay. Bábony, 97 Petőfi Sándor utca
— The Gyula Rudnay Memorial Museum, 97 Petőfi Sándor utca

KAPOLY
— Roman Catholic Church, Baroque (14th c., renovated in 1777). Rococo interior. Altarpiece by János Vaszary (1867–1939): St. Michael, 58 Szabadság utca

KEREKI
— Castle ruin, the so-called Soldier Castle. (Fehérkővára). Gothic (early-14th c.), at a height of 283 m.
— Roman Catholic Church, Neo-Classic (1830)

ZICS
— Roman Catholic Church, late Baroque (1876). Croft and nave ceiling picture by the Vienna master J. Dorfmeister (1725–1797). Baroque furnishings. Dózsa György utca

IGAL
— Spa, with medicinal water containing iodine, bromine and sulphur, at temperatures of 80 C and 52 C. It is used as a cure for locomotor disorders.

TELEKI
— Roman Catholic chapel, with Romanesque croft (13th c.) and Baroque nave (18th c.). Cemetery at Kevei dűlő

LÁTRÁNY
— Church ruin, Romanesque style (first half of 13th c.). Rádpuszta.
— Roman Catholic Church, Baroque (1763). Baroque interior. 10 Vörös Hadsereg utca

SOMOGYTÚR
— Former Bosnyák Manor, Neo-Classic (c. 1830). Next to it the Lajos Kunffy Picture Gallery. 22 Árpád utca.
— Ornamental park

KARÁD
— Folk Centre. The exhibited material presents the folk art of Karád: embroidery and dress. 4 Attila utca

SZŐLŐSKISLAK
— Wine Museum in the one-time Jankovich Manor

SZŐLŐSGYÖRÖK
– Former Jankovich Palace, Neo-Classic (*c.* 1820). Rebuilt in the Romantic style (*c.* 1860), it is surrounded by a protected arboretum

LENGYELTÓTI
– Tóti-Lengyel Palace, Rococo (18th c.), with arboretum in its garden
– Horváth Palace (late 17th c.)

SOMOGYVÁR ·
– Somogyvár Historical Memorial Place
– Ruins of St. Giles' basilica and Benedictine Abbey, Romanesque style (1091–1095 and 12th–13th c.), Kupa-Várhegy.
– Former Széchenyi Palace, early-eclectic (1855, enlarged 1870, converted in 20th c.). Protected garden. 4 Kaposvári u.

BUZSÁK
– Roman Catholic Church, Baroque (second half of 18th c.). Louis XVI-style furnishings, adorned with famous Buzsák embroidery. Petőfi utca
– Folk Centre. The folk art of Buzsák. 7 Tanács tér
– Csisztapuszta baths. Water at 42 C. Used for locomotor disorders. On the outskirts.

NIKLA
– Dániel Berzsenyi Memorial Museum, former Berzsenyi Manor. Neo-Classic (1811). 96 Berzsenyi utca
The sepulcher of the poet Dániel Berzsenyi (1776–1836), 1859. At the cemetery.

ÖREGLAK
– Roman Catholic Church, Neo-Classic (first half of 19th c.). Baroque interior. Fő utca
– Roman Catholic chapel, late Baroque (18th c.). 12 Vasút utca, Nagyhegyszőlő

NORTHERN SHORE

BALATONAKARATTYA
– So-called Rákóczi Tree, 400 year-old elm. One-time county border

BALATONKENESE
– Calvinist Church, Gothic steeple, the rest Baroque (18th c.). Táncsics Mihály utca
– Thatch-roofed csarda-inn and local history collection. One-time dwelling (1857). 25 Táncsics Mihály utca
– Roman Catholic Church, late Baroque (1819). Táncsics Mihály utca

– Tartar Holes. Medieval "cave abodes" carved into the embankment
– "Tátorján". A rare protected plant species on the embankment

BALATONFŰZFŐ
– Ruins of the Church of Máma, Romanesque (13th c.). 37 Jókai utca
– Romkút Spring, sections of the foundations walls of a Roman villa. Popular excursion spot.

BALATONALMÁDI – VÖRÖSBERÉNY
– Roman Catholic Church, Baroque (1777–1779), with Baroque murals inside. Next to it stands a former Jesuit monastery. Vörösberény, 7 Veszprémi utca
– Calvinist Church, a fort church of Romanesque-Gothic origin (13th c., converted in the 18th–19th c.). Vörösberény, Veszprémi út.
– Baroque granary (18th c.). Vörösberény, 1 Rákóczi u.
– The bust of Sándor Petőfi. By Miklós Izsó (end of 19th c.). Nagypark
– Chapel dedicated to the Holy Dexter of St. Stephen. Glass mosaic by Miksa Róth (1865–1944) in the croft
– Miklós Wesselényi lookout tower. At a height of 296 m, with tourist hostel.

ALSÓÖRS
– Calvinist church, Romanesque in origin, with 15th c. details, converted in 1788. Louis XVI furnishings, *c.* 1780. Úttörő utca
– The so-called "Turkish Tax-collecting House", a Gothic manor house (turn of 15th and 16th centuries, converted in 1880.). 4 Petőfi köz

FELSŐÖRS
– Former Roman Catholic Provost Church, Romanesque style (first half of 13th c.), converted in the Baroque style (1749). Interior: Romanesque stone baptising well (first half of 13th c.), additional objects in the Baroque and Rococo style. Dózsa tér
– Provost's House, Baroque (first half of 18th c.). Today houses a library, museum and the Old Lion Restaurant. 3 Dózsa tér
– Former Köves Manor, late Baroque (1792). 3 Szabadság utca

PALOZNAK
– Roman Catholic Church, Romanesque style (13th c.), rebuilt, enlarged in the Neo-Classic style (1835)

CSOPAK

- Ruins of St. Nicholas's Church, Romanesque (13th c.), 41 Kossuth utca
- Calvinist Church, late Baroque (1800). Paloznaki utca
- Cave Tower, rebuilt in the Baroque style from the remnants of a Gothic church (18th c.). 102 Kossuth utca
- Water-mill on Nosztori Brook. (19th c.). Mill Museum, mill-history exhibition.
- Vintner's House. Folk monument. Bereghát
- Dwelling House. Folk monument (mid-19th c.). 89 Füredi utca
- Former Ranolder Villa, Romantic (c. 1860). 12 Kishegy utca
- Press House, mural inside. Folk monument. 5 Füredi utca

BALATONFÜRED

- Former Jókai Villa, early-eclectic (c. 1870), now the Jókai Memorial Museum. Collections: documents on the life of this great Hungarian writer. 1 Honvéd utca
- So-called Horváth House, Louis XVIth style (1798), now a sanatorium. 1 Gyógy tér
- Roman Catholic Round Church, Neo-Classic (designed by Antal Fruman, 1841–1846). Blaha Lujza utca
- State Hospital, Cardiatric House. Gyógy tér
- Calvinist Church, Neo-Classic (1829). Kossuth utca
- Former Gombás Manor, Louis XVI-style (end of 18th c.). 94 Arácsi utca
- Lajos Kossuth Drinking Hall, Neo-Classic (Mátyás Lechner, 1800, rebuilt in 1853). Gyógy tér
- Tagore Walk, with 12 memorial trees
- Yacht harbour
- Lóczy Cave. Öreghegyi út
- Noszlopy look-out point, Recsek Hill, 430 m
- Koloska Valley and csarda-inn, riding school
- Kéki Valley
- Jókai look-out tower
- Former Blaha Manor, Neo-Classic (1816). 2 Blaha Lujza út
- Former Dőry Villa, Romantic (1869). 26 Jókai utca
- Cemetery, church ruin. Romanesque style on Roman foundations, later Gothic (12th and 14th–15th c.). Vázsonyi út
- Residential building, Neo-Classic (c. 1820). 1 Vázsonyi út
- Ferry-man, fisherman. Two bronze statues of János Pásztor (1881–1945). Promenade on the shore
- The Balaton Wind. Statue by Miklós Borsos (1906–1990). Pier

BALATONSZŐLŐS

- Calvinist Church, Gothic (15th c., converted in 1796). Fő utca

TIHANYI FÉLSZIGET – TIHANY

- Roman Catholic Church, formerly of the Benedictine Abbey (1719–1754)
- Tihany Historical Museum, one-time Benedictine Abbey. Medieval in origin, reconstructed several times. Stands next to the Abbey.
- Tihany Open-Air Ethnographical Museum. Sales House of Folk Art, peasant house with chimneyless kitchen (c. 1800), house of a fishermen's guild from Disznós. 20 Batthyány utca, Halász köz, 11 Pisky sétány. Potter's house. 9 Pisky sétány, 26 Batthyány utca
- Statue of St. John of Nepomuk, Baroque (c. 1730). Csokonai liget
- Calvinist Church, late Baroque (1793) and woodden belfry (1888). Tihany, Batthyány utca
- The peasant dwellings of the ancient village: in Petőfi, Csokonai and Kossuth utca
- The Inner Lake
- The Golden House geiser cone
- The Tihany ferry crossing
- Club Tihany, a holiday village
- Church ruin in Újlak, Romanesque (13th c.)
- Recluses' Caves, the so-called monk dwellings. Monks cells carved into rock (11th c.). On the eastern side of the peninsula
- Földvár (Iron Age)

ASZÓFŐ

- Church ruin, Romanesque style (13th c.), with Gothic choir (15th c.)

ÖRVÉNYES

- Church ruin, Romanesque (13th c.). Cemetery
- Upper Mill. Functioning water-mill (13th c., converted at the beginning of the 19th c.)
- Bridge with the statue of St. John of Nepomuk, late Baroque (c. 1800)
- St. Emergy, Roman Catholic church, late Baroque (1778–1783). Templom tér
- Remains of Roman settlement (1st–4th c.). Hosszúrétek-dűlő

BALATONUDVARI

- Calvinist Church, late Baroque (c. 1780). Kerkápoly utca
- Roman Catholic Church, Romanesque style (13th c.), rebuilt in the Neo-Classicist style (c. 1840). Along the high-road
- Heart-shaped tombstones, folkish Baroque (1800–1841). Cemetery alongside the Balaton motorway

PÉCSELY
- Pusztavár, Zádorvár, Gothic (1384). Zádori dűlő
- Folkish press houses on the wine hill from the last century

BALATONAKALI – DÖRGICSE
- Roman Catholic Church, built partly with the walls of the Romanesque church (1787, renovated 1827). Dózsa György út
- Church ruin, Romanesque style (11th–12th c.), the part added to it dates from the first half of the 13th c. Felsődörgicse
- Baroque stone bridge (13th c.). Kisdörgicse
- Lajos Kossuth look-out tower. Halom-hegy, Kű-völgy

ZÁNKA
- Calvinist Church, Romanesque style (13th c., converted 1785–1786, 1879). Fő utca
- Wall remains from the Francovian Era. Hegyestű

BALATONCSICSÓ
- Roman Catholic Church and parish house, late Baroque (1799, reconstructed). 17 Fő utca
- Árokfő: Church ruin in Szentbalázs, Romanesque (13th c., rebuilt in the Gothic style, 14th c.)
- The beech-tree of Csicsó (400–500 years old), now under protection

ÓBUDAVÁR
- Wash-house, folk monument. 32 Fő utca
- Dwelling house, folk monument (1811). 20 Fő utca

MONOSZLÓ
- Ruins of wind-mill
- Calvinist church, Gothic (14th c., converted 1829)
- Calvinist rectory (18th c.)

KÖVESKÁL
- Roman Catholic Church, late Baroque (end of 18th c.). Kossuth utca
- Calvinist Church, Baroque (1769). Bozót utca

BALATONSZEPEZD
- Roman Catholic Church, Romanesque (12th–13th c.), with Gothic parts and Baroque additions (18th c.). Árpád utca
- Memorial column with runic inscription (20th c.). Szepezdfürdő, alongside Road 71.
- Press House, folk monument. Végmál dűlő

RÉVFÜLÖP
- Church ruin, Romanesque style (13th c.). Next to Railway Station
- Local History Collection. 3 Káli utca

KŐVÁGÓÖRS
- Church Ruin, Romanesque style (12th–13th c.), enlarged in the Gothic style (14th–15h c.). Ecséri szőlőhegy
- Church ruin (13th c.). Kisörs
- Lutheran Church, late Baroque on medieval foundations (1811). Jókai utca
- Roman Catholic Church, late Baroque of medieval origin (1773). Jókai utca
- Ruins of Old Christian basilica. Maktyáni dűlő
- Vincellérház, folkish (1843). Fülöphegy
- Homogeneous villagescape, with numerous monuments of folk architecture. Kékkút
- Teodóra Spring, carbonated (sold under the name Kékkúti víz)
- Folk Centre, 19th c. folk dwelling and stable. 55 Fő utca

SZENTBÉKKÁLLA
- Roman Catholic Church, late Baroque (1790–1799). Spire from 1860). Church Hill
- Töttöskáli church ruin, Romanesque style (early 13th c.). On the road leading to the Öreghegy
- Veléte palace ruins, Gothic (14th c.)
- The so-called stone sea. (Peri-glacial blocs)
- Dwarf iris. Massive spring flowering is an extraordinary spectacle
- Dwelling and press-house, folkish. 1 Kishegy utca
- Dwelling house, folkish (1825). 9 Kossuth utca

MINDSZENTKÁLLA
- Roman Catholic Church, Neo-Classic (1829). Rákóczi tér

BALATONRENDES – ÁBRAHÁMHEGY
- Roman Catholic Church, with medieval nave, Baroque croft, rebuilt after 1945. Fő utca
- Press house, folkish (1831). Ábrahámhegy, 84 Iskola utca
- Water-mill, baroque (18th c.). Ábrahámhegy
- Folly Arboretum. Ábrahámhegy

SALFÖLD
- Remains of Roman barrage
- Church and ruins of Paulite monastery, Gothic (14th–15th c.). Örsi hegy
- Roman Catholic Church, Baroque (1769), enlarged (first half of 19th c.), Baroque furnishings

BADACSONY
BADACSONYTOMAJ–BADACSONYTÖRDEMIC
- Badacsony Nature Conservation District
- József Egry Memorial Museum. 52 Egry sétány
- Róza Szegedy House, Baroque (1790). Today it houses the Kisfaludy Memorial Museum for Literature. Kisfaludy út
- Sándor Kisfaludy's press house, Baroque (18th c.). Now a wine bar
- Wine Museum. Yacht House, former Ranolder bishop's summer residence, Hegyalja út
- Badacsonytomaj's basalt church (1932)
- Press house and cellar, folkish, Baroque (1798). 72 Badacsonyi út
- Stone Crucifix, Neo-Classic (1835). Badacsony hill-top
- Statue of Trinity (mid-19th c.). Iskola utca
- Carbonic spring
- Kisfaludy look-out tower. Panorama view
- Outlaws' step. Geological relics on the hill slope
- Local History and Ethnographic Collection. Badacsonytomaj, Fő út
- Gulács, 394 m high. Nemesgulács
- Tóti Hill, 346 m high

SZIGLIGET
- Truncated Tower. Avas church ruin, built with the utilization of Roman-age building, Romanesque style (13th c.)
- Esterházy Palace, Neo-Classic (early-19th c., with 20th c. additions. Today it functions as the resting home of the Hungarian Art Foundation. Its park is protected
- Old Village. Strictly protected area with valuable historical monuments. Numerous peasant abodes and press houses from the 19th century. Kisfaludy utca, Kossuth utca, Petőfi utca
- Castle ruin-Citadel, Roman-age (1260–1262). Converted several times and enlarged up to the 17th c., when it was demolished during the Rákóczi war of independence. Castle Hill
- Lengyel-Putheány Manor, Baroque (1787), converted. Kisfaludy utca
- Arboretum
- "Fox-puller"

BALATONEDERICS
- Roman Catholic Church, built on the site of a Gothic Church in eclectic style (1895). Kossuth utca
- Trinity Statue (1871)
- African hunter's lodge. Endre Nagy's ethnographical and trophy collection from Africa

BALATONGYÖRÖK
- Look-out Tower along the highroad
- Ádám's cellar, folkish (1819). Becehegy
- Major's press house, folkish (1854). Becehegy
- Szántay's press house, folkish (1860). Becehegy

VONYARCVASHEGY
- Saint Crucifix Cemetary Chapel, Neo-Classic (c. 1820). Felszabadulás utca
- St. Michael's Chapel (on medieval foundations, 1622), converted, mural inside (1622), Baroque furnishings. Szentmihály domb
- One-time Festetics Cellar, Neo-Classic (Vilmos Klein, 1819). Today houses the Helikon inn and hotel. Szőlőhegy
- Dwelling houses, folkish (1816). 52 Arany János utca, 65 Zrínyi Miklós utca

GYENESDIÁS
- St. Helen's Chapel, Neo-Classic (1826). Feldiás, cemetery
- So-called Warrior's Cross, Neo-Classic (1807). Alsódiás, Madách utca
- Statue of St. John of Nepomuk (1828). Alsódiás, János Spring
- Darnay's wine cellar, baroque (1644). Felsődiás

KESZTHELY
- Balaton Museum. Collection: the history of Keszthely and the Balaton region, natural and artistic relics. Roman-Age and medieval collection of stonework finds. Folk monuments. 2 Múzeum utca
- Former Festetics Palace: Palace museum and library, cultural centre. Baroque (1745). Southern wing and library (J. Georg and A. Fischer 1792–1800). Chapel (1769–1770). Today's design by E. Hofstadter, 1833–1887. Protected park. 1 Szabadság tér
- Georgikon. The one-time predecessor of the Agricultural University. Louis XVI (1797). 20 Georgikon utca
- Georgikon Manor museum, the farm building complex of the one-time college for agriculture (late Baroque, end of 18th c.). 67 Bercsényi utca
- Amazon hotel and restaurant, late Baroque (c. 1780). 11 Szabadság utca
- Group of historical monuments in the Main Square: Roman Catholic parish, former Franciscan church (1386), next to it a castle (15th to 17th c.) and remains of a chapel (12th–13th c.). The spire of the church from 1896. 15th c. Gothic frescoes in the croft, Trinity statue, Baroque (1770). Building of town council, late Baroque (second half of 18th c.), converted. Former Franciscan, then Premontran monastery, Baroque (1723–1730), converted c. 1800, and 20th c. Today it houses a youth dormitory

– So-called Simon House, Louis XVI (c. 1790). 3 Kossuth utca
– So-called Pethő House, medieval origin, baroque (18th c.), the birthplace of the 19th c. Hungarian composer Károly Goldmark. 22 Kossuth utca
– Helikon Memorial (1954). Dedicated to the great representatives of Hungarian culture in memory of the Helikon Festivities. Helikon park
– Remains of Roman-Age buildings (2nd–6th c.). The area of one-time Roman Valcum–Roman castle, settlement, camp, storage building, Old Christian basilica. Fenékpuszta

HÉVÍZ
– Roman Catholic Church, Romanesque style (13th c.). Converted in 1731. Its painting dates from the 18th c. Egregy, Hegyrétaljai dűlő
– Gyógytó. Hot-water lake. Surface of 47,500 sq.m, temperature of the water 26–33 C. Glass-roofed bathing house. Used to cure locomotor and respiratory disorders
– State Spa Hotel
– Hotel Aqua
– Hotels Hungaria, Napsugár, Béke

REZI
– Roman Catholic Church, Gothic (14th–15th c.). Converted in the Baroque style (1756). Petőfi utca
– Castle ruin (14th c.). Meleghegy, 427 m
– Gyöngyös csárda-inn, Baroque (1728). The Bakony outlaws' one-time favourite haunt. Outlaws' graves nearby

ZALACSÁNY
– Former Batthyány Palace, Baroque (18th c.). Converted in the eclectic style in the second half of the 19th c. 24 Csányi Lajos utca

KALLÓSD
– Roman Catholic Round Church, Romanesque style (second half of 13th c.). Cemetery on the outskirts

LITTLE BALATON AND ITS ENVIRONS

VÖRS
– High look-out with a view of the Little Balaton
– Pedestalled house, peasant abode from 19th c. Ethnographical collection and exhibition entitled Nature Protection on the Little Balaton. 14 Dózsa György út
– Exhibition on the history of fire extinguishing. 1 Flórián tér

BALATONMAGYARÓD – KÁPOLNAPUSZTA
– Buss reserve. The only bull herd in Hungary

ZALAVÁR
– Ruins of castle and abbey. Built at the end of the 11th c. in place of 9th c. castle and church. (Vársziget.) The 9th c. castle is identified with the castle of Pribina, the Slovak leader
– Ruins of a basilica, Romanesque style (11th–13th c.).

RÉCÉSKÚT
– Metod Memorial, a gift from the Bulgarian state

ZALAKAROS
– Spa, health resort, with medicinal water of 96 C

THE ENVIRONS OF NORTHERN BALATON

VESZPRÉM
– Episcopal palace (Jakab Fellner, 1765–1776). There are murals on the facade, in the big hall and chapel, Baroque (second half of 18th c., the work of J. Cymbal). 16 Tolbuhin u.
– Gisela Chapel, early-Gothic (second half of 13th c.). Castle
– Foundations walls of St. George's Chapel, Romanesque (10th–11th and 13th c.). Inside there are traces of murals (13th c.)
– Castle Museum, castle approach, Gate of Heroes
– Former Tejfalussy House, Baroque (1722). The collection of the roman Catholic diocese of Veszprém, treasury. 35 Tolbuhin utca. Also at the same address Museum of Hungarian Architecture–Brick Museum
– Trinity statue, baroque (1749–1751). Castle
– Roman Catholic Church, formerly of the Franciscans, St. Stephen's Church, Louis XVIth style (1723–1730)
– One-time Provost's house, of medieval origin, baroque (1741), housing the fine arts collection of the town of Veszprém. 18 Tolbuhin utca
– Bástya look-out with the statue of St. Stephen and Queen Gisela
– Ruins of the church and convent of Dominican nuns, Gothic (mid-13th c., late-15th c.). 5 Traktor utca
– Former Balassa Manor, Neo-Classic (1817–1819). 9 Budapest utca
– Gábriel Mill, Baroque, of medieval origin, converted in the 18th c. 21 Kittenberger Kálmán utca
– One-time Kapuváry House, late Baroque (1793), converted. 1 Szabadság tér
– Fire Tower. Built on one of the bastions of the medieval castle wall (1772–1814). 31 Tolbuhin utca
– Episcopal cathedral, Romanesque (11th c.-end of 14th c.). Its present form is Neo-Romanesque (1907–1910). Castle

- Piarist Church, Neo-Classic (1828–1833, renovated 1901). 14 Vár utca
- Castle Gallery in the former Dubniczay House, Baroque (1751). 29 Vár utca
- Bakony Museum. The history of the Bakony Mountains and Balaton hill country-exhibition of architecture, history and ethnography. 5 Lenin liget
- Kálmán Kittenberger Plant and Game Park. Fejes-völgy
- Ruins of Veszprém-völgy convent (11th–14th c., built on 10th c. foundations), and the ruins of the 18th c. Baroque Jesuit Church, Baroque (1747). Sallai Imre utca
- Petőfi Theatre, Art Nouveau (1909). Designed by István Medgyaszay. 2 Népköztársaság utca
- Peep-inside-Csarda-inn, late Baroque, 1794. 4 Sallai Imre utca
- Bakony House. The everyday implements of peasant life. 7 Lenin liget

HEREND
- Porcelain factory, late-Neo-Classic (1839), with Museum exhibiting the factory's products. 140 Kossuth utca

ZIRC
- St. Emery's statue. A baroque statue standing on a batch of Roman-Age pillars (c. 1750). Népköztársaság útja
- Roman Catholic, formerly Cistercian Church, Baroque (designed by Márton Witwer and Mátyás Kayr, 1738–1753). Baroque murals by József Wagenmeister (1744–1748). Altar pictures by F. A. Maulbertsch (1754). Baroque furnishings. Rákóczi tér
- Former Cistercian Abbey, Baroque (1727–1732). Neo-Classic facade (1854), Empire library, with marquetry on the furnishings (1820–1830). Protected garden. 1 Rákóczi tér
- Gloriette in the Abbey garden, Baroque (1770)
- Arboretum
- Bakony Museum of Natural Science in the building of the former Abbey. 1 Rákóczi tér. Also here, a Collection of Local History and Ethnography

CSESZNEK
- Castle ruin, Gothic (13th–14th c.). On the outskirts, Castle hill

SÓLY
- Calvinist Church, Romanesque style (13th c.), converted (18th c.)

LITÉR – SZENTKIRÁLYSZABADJA
- Former Tallián-Horváth Palace, Baroque (17th–18th c.), Szentkirályszabadja, Petőfi utca
- Calvinist Church, early-Gothic (end of 13th c.), converted in the baroque style (1784). Unique gate. Litér, Dózsa György utca
- Delapidated well. Ruins of Roman-Age settlement (2nd–4th c.). Szentkirályszabadja

VESZPRÉMFAJSZ
- Baláca garden of ruins and exhibition. Remains of Roman settlement, foundations walls of Roman villas, frescoes, mosaics from the 1st–4th c. Alongside the road between Balácapuszta, Fajsz and Nemesvámos

NEMESVÁMOS
- Roman Catholic Church, Louis XVIth style (early-19th c.). Kossuth utca
- Vámos csárda-inn, folkish, Baroque (second half of 18th c., converted in 1831). Alongside the Veszprém–Nagyvázsony road. Relics of the world of the outlaws

NAGYVÁZSONY
- Kinizsi Castle (14th c. origin, enlarged with 15th c. Gothic parts, rebuilt in 16th–17th c.). There is a Castle Museum in the Keep. Vázsonykő, Kinizsi utca
- Open-air Ethnographical Museum in the so-called Schumacher House (1825)
- Postal Museum. 3 Temető utca
- Former Zichy Palace, Baroque (1762, converted 1815), protected garden. 12 Kossuth utca
- Ruins of Paulite Church and convent, late Gothic (1483). Baráti puszta
- Church ruin, Romanesque (13th c.). Felsőcsepelypuszta
- St. Stephen's Church, Gothic (1401), converted in the baroque style (1773). Rákóczi utca

BARNAG
- St. Florian's statue, Baroque (18th c.). Magyarbarnag
- Calvary Chapel and the Stations of the Corss, Neo-Classic (c. 1800). Németbarnag

MONOSTORAPÁTI
- Roman Catholic Church, Baroque (1759). Baroque murals inside (1786). The work of Ferdinánd Xaverisch. Baroque interior (c. 1760)

TAPOLCA
- Cave with lakes, good access. 7 Batthyány utca
- The memorial collection of the 18th c. Hungarian poet János Batsányi (Tourist Offic). 3 Deák Ferenc utca
- Mill Lake and old water-mill. Today it houses Hotel Gabriella. Batsányi János utca

- Roman Catholic Church with Gothic croft (c. 1400), subsequently Baroque (1757). Szent Imre tér
- Trinity statue, Baroque (18th c.). 4 Batsányi tér
- Stone Bridge, Baroque (18th c.). Embellished
- The so-called Tapolca revolving stage. One of the finest excursion places in the country. Sites: ruins of Megyesd Castle (14th–16th c.). Look-out tower on Boncsos at a height of 447 m, with a view of Monostorapáti. Castle ruins, Romanesque and Gothic in style (13th–14th c.). Csobánc Hill, 376 m, towards Gyulakeszi

HEGYMAGAS

- Szentgyörgy Hill, geological curios, basalt organs, volcanic remains. Nature conservation area
- One-time Lengyel-Tarányi press house, Baroque (c. 1780). Szentgyörgy Hill, on the outskirts
- One-time Sárközy-Márton press house, Baroque (1787). Szentgyörgy-hegy, on the outskirts
- Lengyel Chapel, baroque (1775), Baroque furnishings. Szentgyörgy-hegy
- Uzsa alders. Rare plants, nature conservation area. Lesenceistvánd

LESENCETOMAJ

- Roman Catholic Church, Neo-Classic (1806): In the church there are two Gothic tombstones (1400). Rákóczi tér
- Mammoth pine trees

LESENCEFALU

- Roman Catholic Church with Gothic details, Baroque (1745). Beltelek
- St. Donald's Chapel, Baroque (18th c.). Kápolna dűlő. The view is especially attractive from the chapel
- Kőorra look-out, 401 m. Panorama view

ZALASZÁNTÓ

- Delapidated Tátika Castle, medieval (13th–16th c.). On the outskirts
- Roman Catholic Church. The church of St. Kozma and Damján. Romanesque nave (13th c.). Gothic croft-tower (15th c.), rebuilt in the 18th c. Medieval wall pieces, Gothic, Renaissance and Baroque interior

SÜMEG

- The birthplace of Sándor Kisfaludy, which today houses a memorial museum. Baroque (18th c.), converted at the beginning of the 19th c. Kisfaludy tér
- Roman Catholic Church, formerly Franciscan, Baroque (1652–1657, enlarged 1733, on the basis of plans by Márton Witwer), baroque furnishings. Szt. István tér
- Former bishop's palace (mid-17th c., enlarged c. 1700). Its present form dates from 1748–1755), converted c. 1830. Stucco decoration, baroque wooden panelling. The cellar of the palace houses a wine bar. (Advance notice is necessary for visitors.) 10 Szt. István tér
- Roman Catholic parish church, Baroque. (Design by Márton Witwer, 1756–1757). Baroque furnishings, with murals by F. A. Maulbertsch. Széchenyi utca
- One-time episcopal stables, Baroque (mid-18th c.). Váralja. Agricultural monument, with a model stable with horses inside. Museum of Horse Mountings. Váralja
- Delapidated castle. Built in the 13th c. and rebuilt several times until the 18th c. Today it hosues a museum

TÜRJE

- Roman Catholic Church, formerly of the Premonstratensian provost. Romanesque style (c. 1230, enlarged 1762). In the chapel there are murals by Dorfmeister (1761–1762). Gothic pastoforium, Baroque furnishings.

TOURISM, SPORT, ENTERTAINMENT

ORGANIZED PROGRAMMES

The times indicated here may change from year to year
Information: TOURINFORM; Phone: 117-9800

EXCURSIONS FROM BUDAPEST TO LAKE BALATON

Balaton
Full-day outing. Journey by coach to Tihany to see the sights of the peninsula. Lunch in Badacsony. Bathing and pleasure-boating on the lake. In the afternoon a tour of Balatonfüred and wine-tasting in a csarda-inn
Departures: 1 May–31 October, 8.00 am Mondays and Thursdays. Coaches leave from the Central Coach Terminal (Budapest, V., Engels tér), from the IBUSZ platform

Badacsony Grape Harvest
A midday meal accompanied by gipsy music awaits visitors in Badacsony. This is followed by a boat trip on Lake Balaton. Champagne is served on the ship. In the afternoon, visitors themselves may pick the ripe grapes and drink as much must and wine as they like. In the evening follows a grape harvest feast, with performances by a dance ensemble and a raffle.
Departures: 1 September–31 October, 9.00 am Saturdays. Coaches leave from the Central Coach station (Budapest, V., Engels tér), from the IBUSZ platform

A Day-Trip to Balaton
Arrival to Siófok in the early-morning hours, where guests will see an exhibition presenting the minerals of the Carpathian Basin. Then follows a visit to the Szántódpuszta manor museum, and to an equestrian show. Lunch is at Kőröshegy, then follows a visit to the 15th c. monument church. In the afternoon there is bathing in the lake.
Groups should apply to the SIOTOUR Travel Agency, Budapest, VII., Klauzál tér 2–3.; Phone: 112-6080

EXCURSIONS TO THE BALATON ENVIRONS

Hévíz–Keszthely–Badacsony
Full-day excursion. Parties leave in the morning from Balatontourist offices and campsites. In the morning there is bathing in the famous Termál Baths of Hévíz. This is followed by lunch at a good restaurant, then comes a visit to

Keszthely and the unique Baroque Festetics Palace. In the afternoon wine tasting and dinner Hungarian style awaits visitors
Apply to local branches of BALATONTOURIST

Veszprém–Herend–Zirc
Visitors will arrive to Veszprém in the morning, where they will see the famous sights of the Castle District, the Bakony Museum and the Zoo. After lunch there is a visit to the Museum of the porcelain factory. At Zirc, the Reguly Library awaits them, with a walk in the Arboretum concluding this outing
Apply to local branches of SIOTOUR

Tihany–Nagyvázsony–Tapolca–Keszthely
Crossing the Balaton by ferry. In Tihany there is a visit to the Abbey and the artisans' houses. In Nagyvázsony a trip to Kinizsi Castle, in Keszthely to the Festetics Palace, the Balaton Museum and the Franciscan Church are in the planned programme.
Apply to the local SIOTOUR branches

Szántódpuszta
Visits to the 18th c. monument complex and exhibitions at the Centre for Tourism and culture. This is followed by lunch at the Ménes csarda-inn, then follows carriage-riding and the return journey.
Departures: May to September, on demand, at 9.00 a.m. on any day
Parties leave from Siófok, from the Hotel Hungaria and the Vadvirág summer colony, Balatonszemes
Apply to the main SIOTOUR office, Siófok, Szabadság tér 6.; Phone: 84/10-801

Historical equestrian show at Nagyvázsony
The 3-day event is held annually in remembrance of King Matthias Corvinus. The programme includes medieval historic plays, fairs, theatrical performances and equestrian shows.
Date: 2–5 August, 1990.
Information: BALATONTOURIST Central Office and Nagyvázsony, Kinizsi Castle

Visit to the Little Balaton Protected Area and Aviary, and medicinal bathing at Zalakaros
Under the guidance of a specialist, visitors may have a look at the rare bird species and their nesting places. Lunch at

a local restaurant, in the afternoon bathing taking the waters at Zalakaros. The programme ends with wine tasting.
Tours start on Tuesday between 19 June and 21 August.
Information: BALATONTOURIST offices

EXCURSIONS FROM LAKE BALATON

Budapest
Full-day outing. Departure from the BALATONTOURIST bureaus and campsites. Breakfast is served on the way, and in the morning there is sight-seeing in Budapest. After visiting the Citadel, there is a tour of the capital including Heroes' Square and the City Park, the Castle District, Matthias Church and the Fisherman's Bastion. Lunch is at a typical Budapest restaurant, then follows a shopping excursion in the Inner City. A Hungarian-style dinner is served on the return journey.
Tours start on workdays between June and September
Apply to local branches of BALATONTOURIST

Outing to the Puszta
Parties depart in the morning from the local branches of BALATONTOURIST or campsites. After breakfast served during the journey, visitors will arrive to Kalocsa, a typical town of the puszta. Brief sight-seeing follows, including visits to the Paprika Museum and he House of Folk Art. This is followed by a Hungarian-style lunch in a local restaurant. In the afternoon there is a carriage-riding excursion and wine tasting. The evening is rounded off with dinner at a wine cellar to the accompaniment of gipsy music.
Tours start on Saturdays and Sundays between 16 June and 26 August
Apply to the local branches of BALATONTOURIST

Szekszárd–Gemenc
In the morning visitors arrive in Szekszárd. Brief sightseeing is followed by an excursion to the Gemenc game reserve, with a visit to the Museum of Hunting. Time will be taken off for a midday meal.
Apply to the local branches of SIOTOUR

Pécs–Mohács
Departure to Pécs in the morning hours. Sightseeing, which includes visits to the Cathedral, the Zsolnay Museum and the Vasarely Museum. The journey then continues with a trip to Mohács, with sightseeing and then a tour of the Historical Memorial Park. (Should this trip coincide with the traditional Carnival festivities, then guests will be able to take part in this full day of merry-making.)
Groups should apply to the local branches of SIOTOUR

BALATON PROGRAMME GUIDE

Sunset Tour
One and a half hours of pleasure yachting on the Balaton. Snacks and champagne are served during the trip.
Departures: in July and August, at 19.15 Tuesdays and Saturdays
Parties leave from Siófok harbour

Pleasure Boat Trip With Dinner
Two and a half hours of pleasure boating on evening Balaton. A gipsy band plays on board, where dinner is also served.
Departures: July and August, 20.00 Fridays
Parties leave from Siófok harbour

Moonlight Party
Two-hour pleasure yachting in July and August. Guests are served snacks and champagne.
Departures: July and August, 21.15 Tuesdays and Saturdays
Parties leave from Siófok harbour

Balaton Fishing
A three-hour outing by ship to become familiar with fishing on Lake Balaton. Good opportunity for photography. A fish dish accompanied by wine is served during this trip.
Depatures: 10.00 daily
Parties leave from Siófok harbour

HUNGARY FOR HEALTH

Hungary is uniquely rich in thermal waters. Bathing and taking the waters was very popular as far back as the Roman age and later, in the Turkish period too.
Thermal waters in Hungary are especially recommended for treating locomotor diseases, gynaecological, digestive, and circulatory disorders. Places best known for their thermal springs are: Budapest, Debrecen, Hajdúszoboszló, Harkány, Hévíz, Szeged, Eger, Gyula, Hódmezővásárhely, Miskolc, Szolnok, Balf, Bükfürdő, Dombóvár, Győr, Igal, Kisvárda, Mezőkövesd, Mosonmagyaróvár, Nyíregyháza, Parádfürdő, Sárvár, and Zalakaros.
In the following we give a brief account of the largest and best equipped medicinal baths and thermal hotels, where specialists await tourists and the sick from all over the world, all the year round.
The central travel bureau for thermal hotels, called *Danubius Szálloda és Gyógyüdülő Vállalat,* is located in Budapest, at 8 Martinelli tér, 1052. Phone: 117-3652, Telex: 22-6343.

WHAT HEALTH RESORTS ARE RECOMMENDED FOR WHAT DISEASES

	Thermal Hotel	Gellért Medicinal Baths	ORFI	Rudas Medicinal Baths	Rác Medicinal Baths	Lukács Medicinal Baths	Császár Medicinal Baths	Király Medicinal Baths	Széchenyi Medicinal Baths	Hévíz	Sárvár	Bükfürdő	Balf	Balatonfüred	Zalakaros	Harkány	Hajdúszoboszló	Parád	Gyula
DISEASES OF LOCOMOTOR ORGANS	●	●	●	●	●	●	●	●		●	●	●	●		●	●	●		●
NERVOUS DISEASES																			
Neuralgia	●	●	●	●						●									
Neuritis	●	●	●							●									
Migraine	●	●	●							●									
Fatigue, stress	●	●	●							●									
DENTAL DISEASES	●	●				●													
HEART DISEASES	●	●							●					●					
GYNAECOLOGICAL DISEASES																			
Menstrual disorders											●	●						●	
Chronic adnexitis										●					●	●	●		
Infertility										●						●			
DISEASES OF THE DIGESTIVE ORGANS																			
Stomach/duodenal ulcers	●												●		●	●			●
Chronic cholecystitis	●		●	●	●								●		●	●			●
Rehab. after stomach/intestine operation	●		●	●									●		●	●	●		
Psychosomatic diseases	●		●	●	●								●		●	●			●
Chronic colitits	●		●	●	●								●		●	●	●		●
Chronic pancreatitis			●																
METABOLIC DISEASES																			
Diabetes	●	●																	
Obesity	●	●																	
OTHER ILLNESSES																			
Kidney stones	●																●		
Chronic tracheitis	●	●	●	●	●	●							●	●			●		
Chronic bronchitis	●	●	●	●									●	●			●		
Chronic laryngitis	●	●	●	●		●							●				●		
SPECIAL CURES																			
"Manager fitness"	●										●	●	●						
Cosmetology — beauty care	●										●	●	●						

Cave Therapy at Tapolca

The extensive cave system of Tapolca, located on the northern shore of Lake Balaton, offers an excellent opportunity for natural cures to people suffering from chronic respiratory disorders and astmathic problems. In a three-week cure, patients spend four hours daily in the world-famous medicinal cave situated under the town hospital, where they rest, take part in physico-therapy and are trained in relaxation methods. Besides medical treatment, the ASPA Pension organizes various activities (tennis, riding, hunting, yachting, wine sampling, pig-killing, etc.).

Apply to the Cave Therapy Section of the Town Hospital *Accomodation* is in the ASPA Pension, in double rooms with shower. (8300, Tapolca, 19 Kossuth L. u. Phone: 87/11-695)

Thermal hotels and spas in the vicinity of Lake Balaton

BÜK – 9740
TERMÁL HOTEL BÜK****
Bükfürdő Phone: 96-13-366
TERMÁL ÜDÜLŐSZÖVETKEZET*
Bükfürdő, 43 Termál krt. Phone: 194
FÜRDŐSZÁLLÓ**
Phone: 94-13-363
KASTÉLY HOTEL (Szapáry Castle)*
9737 Bük, Phone: 105
KÚRIA PANZIÓ
17 Nagy Pál utca, 9730. Phone: 205
BÜKFÜRDŐ CAMPING
Fürdőtelep. Phone: 94-13-363
Open: 1 May–30 Sept.

HÉVÍZ – 8380
THERMÁL****
9–11 Kossuth Lajos utca. Phone: 11-190
THERMAL HOTEL AQUA****
13–15 Kossuth Lajos utca Phone: 11-090
NAPSUGÁR**
3–5 Tavirózsa utca. Phone: 13-208, 13-307.

IGAL – 7275
HŐFORRÁS FOGADÓ (on the campsite)
HŐFORRÁS CAMPING**
Phone: 33
Open: 1 May–15 Sept.

SÁRVÁR – 9600
THERMÁL****
1 Rákóczi út. Phone: 96-16-088
MINI HOTEL*
2 Vadkert utca. Phone: 228, telex: 37-466
THERMÁL CAMPING
1 Vadkert utca. Phone: 292
Open: 1 May–30 Sept.

VADÁSZ KASTÉLY
Vadkert utca. Phone: 45

ZALAKAROS – 8749
TERMÁL ÜDÜLŐTELEP*
Phone: 93-18-202
NAPFÉNY ÜDÜLŐSZÖVETKEZET*
10 Termál utca. Phone: 18-437

SPORTS, HOBBIES

Water Sports

At Balatonfüred, in the XXVII. FICC RALLY camping there is a 800-metre long *electric water-ski track*, suitable for 12 persons simultaneously. The speed can be varied between 30 and 60 km.p.h. The use of life-jackets is compulsory! Open 1 May–31 August, every day 8:00 a.m. to 6:00 p.m. Sailing course at the Balatonalmádi pier. Apply at: BUDAPEST TOURIST, 1052 Budapest, 5 Roosevelt tér. Phone: 117-3555, 118-6167; telex: 22-5726.
Sellő Yacht Club, 8630 Balatonboglár pier.
Hiring of sailboats: at the Balatonboglár and Balatonalmádi pier, or BALATONTOURIST Veszprém, 3 Münnich Ferenc tér. Phone: 80/13-750; telex: 32-350.
MAHART Balatoni Hajózási Leányvállalat, 8600 Siófok, 2 Krúdy sétány, Phone: 84/10-050, telex: 22-5805
Hiring of surf-boards and *waterbikes:* in the major campsites and beaches at Lakes Balaton and Velence, and in the campsites of Express Travel Bureau: Balatonszemes, Kiliántelep, and Velence. *Surfing* courses are organized by Express Youth Travel Bureau, Budapest V, 4 Semmelweis utca. Phone: 117-8600, telex: 22-7108

Rowing, Canoeing

The most suitable waters for water tourism are the Rivers Danube and Tisza, Rába and the Körös rivers, as well as Lakes Balaton and Velence. Further information: Magyar Természetbarát Szövetség, Information Office, Budapest, VI, 31 Bajcsy-Zsilinszky út. Phone: 111-2467, 111-9289, or at the county offices.

Angling

Hungary is rich in waters suitable for angling. Tourists must show their passports for fishing permits. Information: MOHOSZ – (Hungarian National Angling Association), 1051 Budapest, 20 Október 6. utca. Phone: 132-5315, from Monday to Thursday 8:00 a.m. to 5:00 p.m., Friday 8:00 a.m. to 4:00 p.m. Occasional angling tickets are sold in travel agencies, tourist offices, hotels, campsites and at the local offices of the Association.

Tennis Courts

Balatonalmádi, Auróra és Tulipán Szállodák
Balatonföldvár, Neptun Szálloda
Balatonfüred, Marina Szálloda
Balatonfüred, camping
Aszófű, Séd camping
Balatonszárszó, Szabadidő Club, Strand
Balatonszemes, Vadvirág Nyaralótelep

Kiliántelep, Ifjúsági Tábor
Révfülöp, Napfény Camping
Siófok, Szállodasor
Siófok, Szabadidő Klub
Tihany, Club Tihany
Keszthely, Castrum camping
Keszthely, Helikon Szálloda
Boglárlelle, Sellő Camping
Héviz, Aqua Szálló
private tennis courts in most places

Horse Riding

Gallopping races are open from spring till autumn on Thursday and Sunday afternoons, at Budapest X, 2 Dobi István út. Trotting races are open all the year round on Wednesdays at 4:30 p.m., and Saturdays at 2:00 p.m. at Budapest VIII, 9 Kerepesi út, near the Eastern Railway Station. Tourist offices and travel agencies both organize riding tours. Hungary has some of the best cross-country riding tracks in Central-Europe. For riding tours contact: IBUSZ (Budapest V., 5 Felszabadulás tér); SIOTOUR (8622 Szántódpuszta. Phone: 84/31-014); BALATONTOURIST (8291 Nagyvázsony. Phone: 80/64-318), and PEGAZUS TOURS (Budapest V., 5 Károlyi Mihály utca. Phone: 117-1552, 118 0542)

Riding schools

Balatonalmádi, Kerekes Vendégfogadó – 60 Mátyás király u.
Balatonfenyves, 1 Nimród u. Phone: 84/61-411
Hévíz, Aqua Szálloda
Keszthely, Helikon Szálló
Keszthely, Castrum camping
Keszthely, Lovasiskola – Phone: 12-408
Nagyvázsony, Kastély Szálló
Nagyvázsony, Lovasiskola – 10 Kossuth L. u.
Phone: 80/31-029
Örvényes, Lovasiskola
Siófok, Idegenforgalmi Hivatal
Szántódpuszta, Idegenforgalmi és Kulturális Központ
Szentbékkálla, Pegazus Fogadó – Phone: Köveskál 10
Taliándörögd, Lovas Fogadó
Phone: 87/11-855

Hunting

The forests of Hungary abound in game. Information on hunting may be obtained from:
HUNTOURS
1024 Budapest, 34 Retek utca. Phone: 135-2313
MAVAD
1014 Budapest, 39 Úri utca. Phone: 155-6715, telex: 22-5965
VADEX (Foreign Trade Office of the Mezőföld State Forestry)

1013 Budapest, 41–43 Krisztina körút (in Hotel Buda-Penta).
Phone: 166-7652, 161-0060, telex: 22-7653
PEGAZUS TOURS – VADCOOP
1052 Budapest, 4 Apáczai Csere János utca (in Hotel Duna Inter-Continental). Phone: 117-5122, telex: 22-5277

Hiking

Information on guided tours and walks:
Magyar Természetbarát Szövetség.
Information: Phone: 153-1930
Budapest VI., 31 Bajcsy-Zsilinszky út II/3.
Postal address: 1374 Budapest, 5. P.O.Box 614.
Phone: 111-2467, 111-9289 or
Budapesti Természetbarát Szövetség
1364 Budapest V., 62–64 Váci utca. P.O.Box 29.
Phone: 118-3933 ext. 58.

Stamp-Collecting

Stamp-collecting is a very popular hobby in Hungary. Purchase and sale: Magyar Filatéliai Vállalat, which has two shops in Budapest VI., 3 November 7. tér, and V., 17–19 Petőfi Sándor utca. There are shops also in major country towns and country seats. Stamps may be taken out of the country with the special permission of the customs office only. Information at any customs office. Hungarian collectors may send stamps abroad up to the value of 6,000 Forints a year. Exchange and customs formalities: Magyar Bélyeggyűjtők Országos Szövetsége, Budapest VI., 65 Vörösmarty utca.

Buying Art Objects

The Bizományi Áruház Vállalat is at your disposal: Budapest IX., 12 Kinizsi utca, headquarters. Phone: 117-6511. There is a huge network of shops selling art objects, paintings, carpets, furniture. The above enterprise also provides information customs regulations and the export of art.

Numismatics

Hungary has a rich tradition of medal and coin collecting. The Magyar Éremgyűjtők Egyesülete (Numismatic Association of Hungary) organizes several auctions a year. Their address: Budapest VI., 77 Népköztársaság útja. Phone: 122-3667. Export or exchange of old coins, medals, badges and decorations can be arranged through the National Bank of Hungary.

GOURMETS' DELIGHTS

Attractive restaurants, wine-cellars and inns offer delicious food and drinks – a real challenge to the palate!

A characteristic spice of Hungarian cuisine is paprika, the small, aromatic red pepper. Sour cream is used with many dishes, giving them a special flavour.

The best-known and most popular Hungarian dishes are kettlegoulash (bográcsgulyás), fish-soup (halászlé), chicken fried in batter, meat roasted on a skewer, and all kinds of wild game. Roast pike-perch (fogas) is always a real Hungarian treat.

Among the delicious Hungarian dessert offerings are apple, sweet cheese, cherry and cabbage strudel. Filled crêpes are also popular. Dobos cake – named after its "inventor", a Hungarian confectioner – is known throughout the world. Tasty Hungarian wines top off the meal. Of these the most renowned is Tokay Aszú, the "wine of kings and the king of wines" ever since the Middle Ages. Other wines that should be tasted are the white are Badacsonyi Kéknyelű, Rizling and Szürkebarát, and Egri Bikavér, a heavy red wine.

RESTAURANTS

ALSÓÖRS – 8226
HALÁSZTANYA
7 Vörös Hadsereg útja (Phone: 86/47-002)
VÉN OROSZLÁN
3 Dózsa tér

BADACSONY – 8261
HALÁSZKERT
5 Park utca (Phone: 87/31-054)
KISFALUDY HÁZ
87 Szegedy Róza út
BORMÚZEUM RESTAURANT
6 Hegyalja út (Phone: 87/31-262)
SZŐLŐSKERT
16 Kossuth Lajos utca (Phone: 87/31-248)
VÍG BACCHUS
26 Kossuth Lajos utca (Phone: 87/31-543)
BAZALT
Badacsonytomaj, 7 Fő utca

BALATONALMÁDI – 8220
KÉK BALATON
27 József Attila utca (Phone: 86/39-013)
KEREKES
60 Mátyás király utca
BUDATAVA
1 Taksony utca

BALATONFÖLDVÁR – 8623
NEPTUN
Park (Phone: 84/40-316)
STRAND
11 Rákóczi út (Phone: 84/40-071)
BALATONGYÖNGYE
1 Szentgyörgyi utca (Phone: 84/40-311)

BALATONFÜRED – 8230
BALATON
5 Tagore sétány (Phone: 86/43-092)
HALÁSZKERT
2 Petőfi Sándor utca
HOLSTEN
8 Petőfi Sándor utca
VADÁSZHÁZ
at Koloska Valley

BALATONSZÁRSZÓ – 8624
VÉNDIÓFA
2 Kossuth Lajos utca
LÓKÖTŐ
7 Ady Endre út (Phone: 84/40-208)

BALATONSZEMES – 8636
VIGADÓ
12 Ady Endre út
KISTÜCSÖK

BALATONVILÁGOS – 8171
ALIGA
2 Radnóti Miklós utca (Phone: 84/30-024)
KORMORÁN
Rákóczi út

BOGLÁRLELLE – 8638
ZÖLD LUGAS
4 Honvéd utca (Phone: 84/50-379)
KINIZSI
2 Vörösmarty tér
SIESTA
108 Dózsa György út (Phone: 84/50-019)
ALBATROSZ
291/a Rákóczi út (Phone: 84/51-744)

CSOPAK – 8229
NOSZTORI
97 Kossuth Lajos utca (Phone: 86/46-100)

FONYÓD – 8640
SIRÁLY
3 Bartók Béla út
PRÉSHÁZ
17 Lenke utca
GYÖNGYHALÁSZ
1 Fürdő utca

HÉVÍZ – 8380
DEBRECEN
3 Rákóczi út (Phone: 12-877)
RÓZSAKERT
19 Rákóczi út (Phone: 12-035)
PIROSKA
10 Kossuth Lajos utca (Phone: 12-698)
BADACSONY
7 Kossuth Lajos utca (Phone: 13-280)

KŐRÖSHEGY – 8617
MUSKÁTLI
90 Petőfi utca (Phone: 84/40-043)

KESZTHELY – 8360
AMAZON
11 Szabadság út (Phone: 12-392)
HUNGÁRIA
35 Kossuth Lajos utca (Phone: 12-265)
BÉKE
50 Kossuth Lajos utca (Phone: 12-447)
JUVENTUS
1 Mártírok útja (Phone: 12-986)
GEORGIKON
Fő tér (Phone: 11-453)

NAGYVÁZSONY – 8291
VÁZSONYKŐ
84 Kinizsi utca (Phone: 80/31-025)
VÁZSONY
(Phone: 80/64-152)

SIÓFOK – 8600
FOGAS
184 Fő utca (Phone: 84/11-405)
KÁLMÁN IMRE RESTAURANT
Kálmán Imre sétány
CSÁRDÁS
105 Fő utca (Phone: 84/10-642)
EURÓPA
15 Kálmán Imre utca

TAPOLCA – 8300
TAVASBARLANG
24 Arany János utca (Phone: 87/11-446)
BÉCSI PINCE
1 Kisfaludy utca (Phone: 87/12-578)
BALATON
2 Deák Ferenc utca (Phone: 87/12-164)

TIHANY – 8237
VITORLÁS FOGADÓ RESTAURANT
Halásztelep (Phone: 86/48-399)
HALÁSZTANYA
11 Visszhang út
SPORT
34 Fürdőtelep (Phone: 86/48-251)
MATRÓZ
Rév (Phone: 86/48-003)

VESZPRÉM – 8200
MAGYAROS
6 Kossuth Lajos utca (Phone: 80/13-060)
VADÁSZTANYA
22 József Attila utca (Phone: 80/12-495)
ERDEI KISVENDÉGLŐ
Vadaspark (Phone: 80/13-085)

INNS, WINE-CELLARS

BADACSONY – 8261
PANORÁMA BORPINCE
14 Hegyalja út (Phone: 87/31-593)
PIROSKA BORHÁZ
on the Badacsony-hill

BALATONAKALI – 8243
MANDULA CSÁRDA
at the highway

BALATONEDERICS – 8312
RÉPA ROZI CSÁRDA
Törökpuszta

BALATONFÖLDVÁR – 8623
KUKORICA CSÁRDA
53 Budapesti út (Phone: 84/40-387)

BALATONFÜRED – 8230
BARICSKA CSÁRDA
Baricska dűlő (Phone: 86/43-105)

HORDÓ CSÁRDA
Baricska dűlő (Phone: 86/43-417)
KOLOSKA CSÁRDA
Koloska Valley
KALÓZ CSÁRDA
5 Zalka Máté utca (Phone: 86/42-006)

BALATONGYÖRÖK – 8313
PANORÁMA CSÁRDA
BECEHEGYI CSÁRDA
Becehegy

BALATONKENESE – 8174
ZSINDELYES CSÁRDA
25 Táncsics Mihály út

BOGLÁRLELLE – 8638
BECSALI CSÁRDA
80 Rákóczi utca (Phone: 84/51-416)
KINIZSI UDVAR
2 Vörösmarty tér (Phone: 84/50-509)

CSOPAK – 8229
MALOM CSÁRDA
Nosztori Valley
VÍG MOLNÁR CSÁRDA
at highway

FONYÓD – 8640
PRÉSHÁZ CSÁRDA
7 Lenke utca

FELSŐÖRS – 8227
PATKÓ CSÁRDA
Öreghegy

HÉVÍZ – 8380
GYÖNGYÖSI CSÁRDA
at Rezi
VADASKERT CSÁRDA
Between Keszthely and Hévíz (Phone: 12-772)

KESZTHELY – 8360
HALÁSZCSÁRDA
Balatonpart (Phone: 12-751)

KŐRÖSHEGY – 8617
FLEKKEN CSÁRDA
Dózsa György út (Phone: 84/40-048)

NEMESVÁMOS – 8248
BETYÁR CSÁRDA

RÉVFÜLÖP – 8253
BIRKA CSÁRDA
17 Füredi út

SIÓFOK – 8600
PIROSKA CSÁRDA
Fokihegy (Phone: 84/10-683)
BORHARAPÓ CSÁRDA
34 Fő út

SZÁNTÓD – 8622
RÉV CSÁRDA
(Phone: 84/31-157)
MÉNES CSÁRDA
Szántódpuszta

TIHANY – 8237
KECSKEKÖRÖM CSÁRDA
13 Kossuth Lajos utca

ZAMÁRDI – 8621
PAPRIKA CSÁRDA
1 Honvéd utca

NIGHT CLUBS, DISCO CLUBS

BADACSONY – 8261
TROPICAL DISCO
Badacsonytomaj, 1 Vasút utca
IL CAPITANO NIGHT CLUB
(Phone: 87/31-292)

BALATONALMÁDI – 8220
PANORÁMA CLUB
1 Wesselényi park (Phone: 80/38-822)

BALATONFÖLDVÁR – 8623
KERINGŐ
9 Hősök útja (Phone: 84/40-192)

BALATONLELLE – 8638
RÓZSAKERT NIGHT CLUB
30 Honvéd utca

BALATONFÜRED – 8230
TÜKÖR BÁR
Huray út (Phone: 86/42-006)

HELKA HAJÓBÁR
METAL FUNKY ROCK DISCO

KESZTHELY – 8360
AMAZON NIGHT CLUB
11 Szabadság út (Phone: 12-392)
URÁNIA DRINK
2 Jókai utca
HELIKON BAR

RÉVFÜLÖP – 8253
IBOLYA DISCO
1 Halász utca

SIÓFOK – 8600
BABYLON CLUB
(Phone: 84/10-632)
PIPACS BAR
11 Mártírok útja
EUROPA BAR
17 Petőfi sétány (Phone: 84/13-411)
ÉDEN BAR
15 Petőfi sétány (Phone: 84/10-665)
ARIZONA BAR
14 Batthyány utca (Phone: 84/10-654)
CSIKÓ BAR
Petőfi sétány (Phone: 84/10-652)

CASINO HÉVÍZ
– at Hotel Thermal (9–11 Kossuth Lajos utca)
French and American roulette, Black Jack, gambling machines

A GUIDE TO EVENTS AT LAKE BALATON AND TRANS-DANUBIA

MAY
Siófok–Balatonfüred
Opening of the Balaton season – national choir festival, folk art fair, sports events, yacht race

JUNE
Őriszentpéter
Őrség fair – folk art exhibits, fairs
Szántódpuszta
Equestrian days, programmes of entertainment
Szombathely
International dance contest and Hungarian championships

JUNE–AUGUST
Tihany
Organ concerts in the Abbey Church

Szántódpuszta
St. Jacob's Day Fair, folk art fair and programmes

JULY
Győr
Győr Summer – Theatrical performances, concerts of serious and light music, fairs of folk applied art, folklore performances, ballet
Pécs
Pécs Summer Theatrical Days – folk dance productions on the open-air dance-house stage, literary recitals in the Anna Courtyard, theatrical performances at the Tettye Ruins, concerts in the Cathedral
Balatonfüred
International Anna Ball
Boglárlelle
Boglár Summer Theatre
Keszthely
Chamber Music concerts in the music hall of the Festetics Palace, organ concerts in the Carmelite Church

JULY–AUGUST
Kőröshegy
Organ concerts
Buzsák
Buzsák fair, folklore programmes
Nagyvázsony
Nagyvázsony equestrian games
Veszprém
Veszprém Musical Courtyard, Veszprém Folk Art Fair, Potters' Fair

AUGUST
Boglárlelle
Boglár grape harvest
Felsőörs
Concerts of chamber music in the Roman Catholic Church
Siófok
Concerts in the Roman Catholic Church

SEPTEMBER–OCTOBER
Badacsony
Grape harvest merry-making, wine auction
Somló
Grape harvest festivities, folk art fair

OCTOBER
Museum month – exhibitions, special events throughout the country
Grape harvest festivities in several provincial towns

ACCOMMODATIONS

HOTELS AT LAKE BALATON

ALSÓÖRS – 8226
HOTEL PELIKÁN**
62 Vörös Hadsereg út; Phone: 86/47-149

BALATONALMÁDI – 8220
AURÓRA HOTEL***
Bajcsy-Zsilinszky út; Phone: 86/38-810
Open: V. 1.–IX. 30.
TULIPÁN SZÁLLODA**
1 Marx tér; Phone: 86/38-317

BALATONFÖLDVÁR – 8623
HOTEL FESZTIVÁL**
35 Rákóczi u.; Phone: 84/40-377
HOTEL NEPTUN***
Phone: 84/40-392
Open: IV. 15.–X. 15.

BALATONFÜRED – 8230
HOTEL ANNABELLA***
25 Beloiannisz u.; Phone: 86/42-222
Open: IV. 20.–X. 14.
HOTEL FÜRED***
20 Széchenyi u.; Phone: 86/43-033
HOTEL MARGARÉTA***
29 Széchenyi út; Phone: 86/43-824
HOTEL MARINA***
26 Széchenyi út.; Phone: 86/43-644
Open: IV. 26–X. 1.
HOTEL ÉDEN***
4 Szabadság u.; Phone: 86/42-111

BALATONMÁRIAFÜRDŐ – 8647
HOTEL MÁRIA***
Phone: 84/76-038

KESZTHELY – 8360
HOTEL HELIKON***
5 Balatonpart; Phone: 11-330
HOTEL HULLÁM***
Balatonpart.; Phone: 12-644
HOTEL PHOENIX**
3 Balatonpart; Phone: 12-630
Open: IV. 1–X. 15.

SIÓFOK – 8600
HOTEL BALATON***
9 Petőfi sétány; Phone: 84/10-655
Open: IV. 28–X. 20.
HOTEL EURÓPA***
15 Petőfi sétány; Phone: 84/13-411
Open: IV. 20.–X. 20.
HOTEL HUNGÁRIA***
13 Petőfi sétány; Phone: 84/10-678
Open: IV. 20.–X. 20.
HOTEL LIDÓ***
11 Petőfi sétány; Phone: 84/10-633
Open: IV. 20.–X. 20.
OKGT ÜDÜLŐSZÁLLÓ**
69–71 Beszédes J. sétány; Phone: 84/11-633
Open: I. 4.–V. 26. and IX. 10.–XII. 15.
VÉNUSZ**
12 Kinizsi u.; Phone: 84/10-660
Open: V. 1.–X. 15.
NAPFÉNY HOTEL**
8 Mártírok u.; Phone: 84/11-408
Open: V. 8.–X. 10.

SZÁNTÓD – 8622
TOURING HOTEL**
Phone: 84/31-096
Open: V. 4.–IX. 30.

TIHANY – 8237
CLUB TIHANY ÜDÜLŐCENTRUM**** and ÜDÜLŐFALU****
3 Rév u.; Phone: 86/48-088
Open: I. 1.–XII. 31.

VESZPRÉM – 8200
HOTEL VESZPRÉM**
6 Budapesti út; Phone: 80/24-876

TOURIST HOTELS, PENSIONS AT LAKE BALATON

BADACSONYÖRS – 8257
SZÜRKEBARÁT FOGADÓ
Phone: 87/31-298

BADACSONYTOMAJ – 8258
EGRY JÓZSEF FOGADÓ
2 Kisfaludy út; Phone: 87/31-057

BALATONALMÁDI – 8223
KRISTÓF MOTEL
2 József A. út; Phone: 80/38-902
KÉK BALATON FOGADÓ
27 József A. út; Phone: 80/39-013

BALATONBERÉNY – 8649
KÓCSAG FOGADÓ
Phone: 84/77-154
Open: VI. 1.–IX. 1.

BALATONEDERICS – 8312
KASTÉLYSZÁLLÓ

BALATONFENYVES – 8646
NYARALÓHÁZ-PARK
12 Hámán Kató út; Phone: 84/61-840
Open: V. 1.–IX. 30.

BALATONFÖLDVÁR – 8623
JUVENTUS HOTEL
6 József A. út; Phone: 84/40-379
Open: IV. 5.–X. 20.
NYARALÓHÁZAK
6 József A. út; Phone: 84/40-379

BALATONFÜRED – 8230
ARANYCSILLAG HOTEL
1 Zsigmond út; Phone: 86/43-466
PANORÁMA PANZIÓ
15 Kun B. út;
RING PANZIÓ
7 Vörösmarty utca; Phone: 86/42-884

BALATONKERESZTÚR – 8648
BÉL MÁTYÁS TÚRISTASZÁLLÓ
26 Ady E. út; Phone: 84/76-180

BALATONMÁRIAFÜRDŐ – 8647
HOTEL TOURING
1 Rákóczi F. út; Phone: 84/76-038
Open: V. 15.–IX. 30.

BALATONSZÁRSZÓ – 8624
TÚRISTASZÁLLÓ és ÜDÜLŐHÁZ
37 Fő út; Phone: 84/40-492
VASMACSKA PANZIÓ
17 József A. utca; Phone: 84/40-493

BALATONSZEMES – 8636
LIDÓ FOGADÓ
53 Ady E. út; Phone: 84/45-112

VADVIRÁG NYARALÓTELEP
Phone: 84/45-115

BALATONSZÉPLAK – 8609
TOURING HOTEL
Balatonszéplak-Felső; Phone: 84/10-684

BALATONUDVARI-KILIÁNTELEP – 8242
ÜDÜLŐHÁZAK
Phone: 86/45-565

BOGLÁRLELLE – 8630
PLATÁN PANZIÓ
56 Hunyadi út; Phone: 84/50-203
IFJÚSÁGI ÜDÜLŐTELEP
Phone: 84/51-537
NAPSUGÁR PANZIÓ
Phone: 84/50-757
SPORT ÜDÜLŐ
Phone: 84/50-482

FARKASGYEPŰ – 8582
BOROSZLÁN FOGADÓ
47 Petőfi út; Phone: 6

FONYÓD – 8640
SIRÁLY SZÁLLODA
3–5 Bartók Béla út; Phone: 89/60-125
NAPSUGÁR ÜDÜLŐHÁZAK, FOGADÓ
5 Komjáth A. út; Phone: 84/61-211
LIGET PANZIÓ
Fonyódliget, Szemere út

KESZTHELY – 8360
AMAZON HOTEL
11 Szabadság út; Phone: 12-248
HELIKON TÚRISTASZÁLLÓ
22 Honvéd utca; Phone: 11-424
ZALATOUR CAMPING-ÜDÜLŐHÁZAK
Balatonpart; Phone: 12-782

KŐRÖSHEGY – 8617
KŐRÖSHEGY FOGADÓ
65 Petőfi u.; Phone: 84/40-508

NAGYVÁZSONY – 8291
KASTÉLY ÉS LOTEL
12 Kossuth út; Phone: 80/64-109
KINIZSI TÚRISTASZÁLLÓ
Vár u.

VÁZSONYKŐ PANZIÓ
2 Sörház út; 80/64-344

RÉVFÜLÖP – 8253
OTTÓ PANZIÓ
29 Kacsajtos út; Phone: 87/44-207

SIÓFOK – 8600
SIÓFOK MOTEL
12 Kinizsi utca; Phone: 84/10-644
TOURING HOTEL FOKIHEGY
Balatonszéplak-Felső; Phone: 84/10-684
Open: III. 24–X. 15.
OÁZIS PANZIÓ
5 Szigliget utca; Phone: 84/13-650

SZÁNTÓDPUSZTA – 8622
PATKÓ FOGADÓ
Phone: 84/31-014

SZENTBÉKKÁLLA – 8281
PEGAZUS LOVASFOGADÓ
39 Kossuth út; Phone: 87/48-164

TALIÁNDÖRÖGD – 8295
LOVAS PANZIÓ
8 Kossuth út; Phone: 87/11-855

TAPOLCA – 8300
GABRIELLA HOTEL
7 Batsányi tér; Phone: 87/12-642
ARTEMISZ PANZIÓ
Tapolca-Diszel: Phone: 87/12-657
ASPA PANZIÓ
19 Kossuth L. utca; Phone: 87/11-695

VONYARCVASHEGY – 8314
KEMPING ÜDÜLŐHÁZ
Szentmihály-domb; Phone: 44
Open: V. 1.–IX. 30.

ZAMÁRDI – 8621
TOURING HOTEL
146 Petőfi út; Phone: 84/31-088
Open: V. 3–IX. 30.

ZIRC – 8420
BAKONY FOGADÓ
1 Rákóczi tér; Phone: 168
BAKONY TÚRISTASZÁLLÓ
1 Rákóczi tér; Phone: 168

BALATON CAMPSITES

ALSÓÖRS – 8226
SZIVÁRVÁNY CAMPING
Phone: 86/47-085

ASZÓFŐ – 8241
DIANA CAMPING
Phone: 86/45-013

BADACSONY – 8261
CAMPING
Phone: 87/31-091

BADACSONYÖRS – 8257
BALATON CAMPING
Phone: 87/31-253

BALATONAKALI – 8243
HOLIDAY CAMPING
Phone: 86/44-514
PACSIRTA CAMPING
4. Pacsirta u.
STRAND CAMPING
Phone: 86/44-513
PRIVAT CAMPING
14 Kossuth L. u.

BALATONAKARATTYA – 8172
PIROSKA CAMPING
15 Aligai út; Phone: 80/81-121

BALATONALMÁDI – 8220
YACHT CAMPING
16 József A. u.; Phone: 86/38-906
KRISTÓF CAMPING
2 Ságvári u.; Phone: 86/38-902

BALATONBERÉNY – 8649
KÓCSAG CAMPING
Gábor Á. u.; Phone: 84/77-154

BALATONEDERICS – 8312
DELTA CAMPING
Kültelek 075.; Phone: 20

BALATONFÖLDVÁR – 8623
MAGYAR TENGER CAMPING
Phone: 84/40-240

BALATONFÜRED – 8230
XVII. FICC RALLY CAMPING
Phone: 86/43-823

BALATONGYÖRÖK – 8313
CARINA CAMPING
12 Balaton u.; Phone: 20

BALATONSZABADI – 8651
IFJÚSÁGI CAMPING
Balatonszabadi-Sóstó; Phone: 84/11-471
GAMÁSZA CAMPING
Phone: 84/30-049

BALATONSZÁRSZÓ – 8624
TÚRA CAMPING
József A. park; Phone: 84/40-254

BALATONSZEMES – 8636
ÉDEN CAMPING
2 Fő u.
VADVIRÁG CAMPING
Phone: 84/45-114
LIDO CAMPING
8 Ady E. u.; Phone: 84/45-112
BAGÓDOMB CAMPING
Phone: 84/45-177
HULLÁM CAMPING
Kasza u.; Phone: 84/45-116

BALATONSZEPEZD – 8252
VENUS CAMPING
Phone: 87/48-048

BOGLÁRLELLE – 8630
SELLŐ CAMPING
3 Kikötő u.
ARANYHÍD CAMPING
53 Köztársaság u.; Phone: 84/50-449

FONYÓD–BÉLATELEP – 8640
NAPSUGÁR CAMPING
5 Komjáth A. u.; Phone: 84/61-211

GYENESDIÁS – 8315
CARAVÁN CAMPING
43 Madách u.; Phone: Keszthely 11-516

KESZTHELY – 8360
ZALATOUR CAMPING
Balatonpart, Phone: 12-782

CASTRUM CAMPING
48 Móra F. u.; Phone: 12-120

PALOZNAK – 8229
NYÁRFA CAMPING
Phone: 86/46-226

RÉVFÜLÖP – 8253
NAPFÉNY CAMPING
5 Halász u.; Phone: 87/44-309

SIÓFOK – 8600
EZÜSTPART CAMPING
Siófok–Balatonszéplak.; Phone: 84/11-374
CAMPING
Siófok-Balatonszéplak, Zichy M. tér; Phone: 84/11-364
KÉK BALATON CAMPING
Darnai tér; Phone: 84/10-851
STRAND CAMPING
Fürdőtelep, 183 Szt. László u.; Phone: 84/11-804
ARANYPART NYARALÓTELEP
Phone: 84/11-801
FŰZFA CAMPING
Szőlőhegy, 4/a Fő u.
IFJÚSÁG CAMPING
Siófok-Sóstó, Pusztatorony tér; Phone: 84/11-471
MINI CAMPING
74 Szent László u.
TOT CAMPING
Fürdőtelep, 19–21 Viola u.

SZÁNTÓD – 8622
RÉV CAMPING
1 Nyár u.; Phone: 84/31-159

VONYARCVASHEGY – 8314
CAMPING
Phone: 44

ZAMÁRDI – 8621
AUTÓS I. CAMPING
Phone: 84/31-163
AUTÓS II. CAMPING
Phone: 84/31-163

TRAVEL BUREAUS, HOTEL AND ACCOMMODATION SERVICE

BALATONTOURIST
1082 Budapest, 52/a Üllői út; Phone: 133-9929

8200 Veszprém, 3 Münnich F. tér; Phone: 80/29-630
Telex: 27-062
8230 Balatonfüred, 5 Blaha Lujza u.; Phone: 86/42-823
Telex: 32-394
8220 Balatonalmádi, 36 Lenin u.; Phone: 80/38-707
Telex: 32-340
8237 Tihany, 20 Kossuth u.; Phone: 86/48-519
8253 Révfülöp, 1 Halász u.; Phone: 87/44-289
8261 Badacsony, 10 Park u.; Phone: 87/31-249
8300 Tapolca, 7 Deák F. u.; Phone: 87/11-179
Telex: 32-657
8420 Zirc, 2 Deák F. u.; Phone: 108
Telex: 32-750
8291 Nagyvázsony, Kinizsi-vár; Phone: 80/64-318
8330 Sümeg, 29 Kossuth u.; Phone: 114

ZALATOUR
Zalaegerszeg 8900, 1 Kovács Károly tér; Phone: 92/11-443
Telex: 33-236
8360 Keszthely, 1 Fő tér; Phone: 12-560
Telex: 35-253

SIÓTOUR
1075 Budapest, 2–3 Klauzál tér; Phone: 112-6080
Telex: 22-4520
8600 Siófok, 2/b Batthyány u.; Phone: 84/13-111
Telex: 22-3044
8600 Siófok, 6 Szabadság tér; Phone: 84/10-900
Telex: 22-4002
8623 Balatonföldvár, 9–11 Hősök u.; Phone: 84/40-099
Telex: 22-7753
8621 Zamárdi, 1 Petőfi u.; Phone: 84/31-072
8638 Boglárlelle II., 1 Szent István u.; Phone: 84/51-086
Telex: 22-6557
8630 Boglárlelle I., 1 Dózsa Gy. u.; Phone: 84/50-665
Telex: 22-6154
8640 Fonyód, Vasútállomás; Phone: 84/61-214
Telex: 22-7400

IBUSZ
1053 Budapest, 5 Felszabadulás tér; Phone: 118-1120
8230 Balatonfüred, 4/a Petőfi Sándor utca; Phone: 86/42-337
Telex: 032-343
8600 Fonyód, 4 Szt. István út; Phone: 84/60-449
Telex: 22-5422
8360 Keszthely, 1–3 Széchenyi út; Phone: 12-951
Telex: 035-305

8600 Siófok, 1–3 Kele utca; Phone: 84/12-011
Telex: 22-6075

EXPRESS IFJÚSÁGI ÉS DIÁK UTAZÁSI IRODA
1052 Budapest, 4 Semmelweis u.; Phone: 117-8600
Telex: 22-7108
1054 Budapest, 16 Szabadság tér; Phone: 131-6393
Keleti Pályaudvar – Budapest; Phone: 142-1772
8200 Veszprém, 6 Kossuth L. u.; Phone: 80/27-069
Telex: 32-402
8360 Keszthely, 22 Kossuth L. u.; Phone: 10-032
Telex: 35-233
8242 Balatonudvari-Kiliántelep; Phone: 86/45-565, 566
Telex: 32-418
8623 Balatonföldvár, 9 József A. u.; Phone: 84/40-303
Telex: 22-5084
Hotel Juventus – 8523 Balatonföldvár; Phone: 84/40-417
Hotel Fesztivál – 8323 Balatonföldvár; Phone: 84/40-374
Telex: 22-7398

BALATONFÜRED TOURIST
8230 Balatonfüred, 8 Petőfi Sándor utca; Phone: 86/42-237
Telex: 03-2442

GENERÁL TOURIST
8220 Balatonalmádi, 134/a Veszprémi u.

KENTAUR TOURIST
8230 Balatonfüred; Phone: 86/42-853
Telefax: 117-6176

MELÓDIA REISEN
8230 Balatonfüred; Phone: 86/43-619
Telex: 32-273

MIDITOURIST
8261 Badacsony, 53 Park u.; Phone: 87/31-028
Telex: 32-271

OMEGA TOURIST
1051 Budapest, 11 József Nádor tér; Phone: 117-2622
Telex: 22-7760

PIROSCHKA
8621 Zamárdi.1Jókai utca; Phone: 84/31-358

PEGAZUS TOURS
1053 Budapest, 5 Károlyi M. u.; Phone: 117-1644
Telex: 22-4679

FURTHER FACTS

ENTRY

Passport, visas
Tourists entering Hungary need valid passports and visas with two photographs.

Visas are issued:
In a foreign country:
– in person at an Embassy
– by post (24 hours)
At the frontier stations:
– by automobile
– at Ferihegy Airport
– at the international boat station ($\frac{1}{2}$ to 1 hour, depending on the traffic).
Prolongation of your visa:
48 hours before the expiration of validity, at the nearest police station. No visas are needed for children under 14 travelling with their parents.

Passport:
Travel documents (passports, visas, statistical leaflets) should be kept by the tourist and presented upon request.
In case of a lost passport:
– call the nearest police station (any time), to issue a temporary document,
– on the basis of the above, your Embassy will issue a new passport,
– an exit visa is needed from the nearest police station.

STAYING IN HUNGARY

Public safety in Hungary is satisfactory. In case of any problems, though, call the police, who will issue documents needed for legal defence.

Registration:
Tourists from the West should register with the police station nearest their temporary residence within 48 hours after entering the country (even in case of a 24-hour stay). Tourist from social ist countries must register only if their stay exceeds 30 days.

CUSTOMS AND EXCHANGE OF FOREIGN CURRENCY

Entry

Duty-free goods
Goods and jewels taken into the country for personal use are duty-free.

Exchange of money
There is no compulsory exchange of money in Hungary. Foreign currency can be exchanged in the National Bank of Hungary, the Országos Takarékpénztár (National Savings Bank), travel agencies, hotels and campings, at the official rate established by the National Bank of Hungary. The document of exchange should be kept until leaving the country.

Travellers cheques
Official places of exchange accept, beside banknotes, travellers cheques and so-called EUROCHEQUEs as well (with a maximum of 9,000 Forints per cheque), issued by the banks of Australia, the US, Holland, France, Iraq, Japan, Jordan, Great Britain, West Germany, Norway, Italy, and Switzerland. These, as well as American Express, Bank of America, Carte Blanche, Diners Club, Eurocard, and Universal Travel Plan cards are accepted in hotels, restaurants, and major supermarkets. If your card is lost, call the Központi Devizapénztár of the National Bank of Hungary, Budapest V., 8–9 Szabadság tér; Phone: 112-3223 or 153-2900. Open: Mondays–Fridays, 9:00 a.m. to 1:00 p.m.

Exit

Re-exchange of Forints
Remaining Forints can be re-exchanged in all major travel agencies and banks, to the maximum of the 50 % of the sum previously exchanged (which sum total, however, should not exceed 100 USD). Be sure to have proof of original exchange!

Goods that may not be taken out of the country
Gold, platinum, silver, and articles made of these materials, as well as art objects. The regulation does not apply to works of art purchased in Intertourist, Konsumtourist and Utastourist shops, with credit cards or convertible currency. For the export of certain goods (foodstuffs, medicine, tools, and textiles), the special permission of the National Bank of

Hungary is required (Budapest V., 8 Szabadság tér, Mondays–Fridays, 8:30 a.m. to 1:30 p.m.). For further information contact: Vám- és Pénzügyőrség, Budapest V., 11/b Szent István tér, Monday–Thursday, 8:00 a.m.–5:00 p.m., on Fridays 8:00 a.m.–4:00 p.m.; Phone: 132-6943

Permission to export art may be obtained from the Hungarian National Gallery, Budapest, Buda Castle, Building 'B'; Phone: 175-7533

TRAVEL

How to reach Hungary

By plane

MALÉV (Hungarian Airlines) has flights to 40 cities in 30 countries. Tickets are sold at MALÉV offices.

Offices in Budapest
Reservation and tickets for MALÉV flights; Phone: 118-4333
1051 Budapest V., 2 Roosevelt tér, Phone: 118-9033
Telex: 22-4954
1051 Budapest V., 2 Dorottya utca; Phone: 118-4333
Telex: 22-5796
Office for Reservation from Abroad:
1051 Budapest V., Roosevelt tér; Phone: 118-5627, 118-1998
Telex: 22-5793.

By rail

30 international trains insure a direct link between Budapest and the major cities of Europe.
Please note: There is no visa service at the railway border crossing points! Passangers should obtain their Hungarian visas prior to departure.
Car trains
The Saxonia Express runs a daily car transport service on the Budapest–Dresden / Dresden–Budapest line during the summer season. (Not available for minibuses and caravans.)

By boat

There is a regular hydrofoil service operating between Budapest and Vienna.
Tickets, reservation, information
In Vienna:
- MAHART Head Office, A-1010 Wien I., Karlsplatz 2/8.
  Phone: 43-222/65-38-44, 65-56-44. Telex: 47/13-1001
- IBUSZ, W-1010 Wien I., Krugerstr. 4.
  Phone: 43-222/51-55-50. Telex: 47/11-1113
- Erste Donau-Dampfschiffahrts-Gesellschaft (DDSG-Reisedienst), A-1010 Wien, Handelskai 265.
Phone: 43-222/26-65-36/55. Telex: 47/13-4789.

By bus

There are regular international bus services between Hungary and seven countries (Austria, Czechoslovakia, Yugoslavia, Poland, FRG, Italy, Soviet Union).
Blaguss-Volánbusz
There is a daily bus service between Budapest and Vienna all the year round.
Dep. 7 a.m. Wien-Mitte, Autobusbahnhof
Arr. 11.35 a.m. Budapest, Engels tér Bus Terminal
Dep. 7 a.m. Budapest, Engels tér Bus Terminal
Arr. 11.35. a.m. Wien-Mitte, Autobusbahnhof.
Tickets, information
IBUSZ Reisen
Offizielles Reisebüro der Ungarischen Staatsbahnen GmbH.
A–1010 Wien I., Kärntnerstr. 26; Phone: 43-222/512-0747.
Telex: 47/11-2282.
Reisebüro Blaguss Reisen
A–1040 Wien, Wiedner Hauptstr. 15;
Phone: 43-222/65-16-81.
Telex: 47/13-3869.
Deutsche Touring GmbH
D–8000 München 2, Arnulfstr. 3; Phone: 49-89/591-824/25.
Telex: 41/05-24990.
Ungarn und Osteuropareisen
D–8000 München 2, Altheiner-Eck 1; Phone: 49-89/265-020.
Telex: 41/05-24585.

By car

The IBUSZ offices at the highway border crossing stations offer visa service, currency exchange and sales of diesel coupons night and day.
Third party insurance is compulsory in Hungary. Registration numbers and international registration letters of the following countries prove that the car has third party insurance: Austria, the Benelux countries, Bulgaria, Czechoslovakia, Denmark, Finland, France, FRG, GDR, Great Britain, Ireland, Liechtenstein, Norway, Poland, Portugal, Spain, Sweden, Switzerland. Green cards are required from motorists of the following countries: Greece, Iceland, Italy, Turkey. Motorists of other countries or motorists with no proof of insurance coverage must take out a temporary third party insurance at the border, which covers them for damage caused to Hungarian citizens in Hungary.

Travel within Hungary

By rail

As there is no domestic flight service in Hungary due to short distances, a considerable part of domestic transport is handled by the railways.

16 express train services operate between the capital and country towns.

Concession available for foreigners:
– group concession (min. 6 persons)
– Balaton season ticket (for 7–10 days)
– tourist season ticket (for 7–10 days)
– senior citizens' ticket for women over 55 and men over 60.

Information on rail travel

In Budapest:
– MÁV Central Information Office, 6 a.m. to 8 p.m.
Domestic travel; Phone: 122-7860, 142-9150
Foreign travel; Phone: 122-4052
– MÁV Passenger Service: Budapest, VI., Népköztársaság útja 35;
Phone: 122-8049, 122-8056
– MÁVTOURS, Budapest, VI., Népköztársaság útja 35;
Phone: 122-8049, 122-8056
Information services of the major railway stations:
Keleti (Eastern) Railway Station; Phone: 113-6835
Nyugati (Western) Railway Station; Phone: 149-0115
Déli (Southern) Railway Station; Phone: 155-8657

By boat
In Budapest
There are regular boat services on the Danube and on Lake Balaton from spring to late autumn, weather permitting. On the Danube, besides the MAHART excursion boats, the Budapest Transport Company also operates ferries in the city centre.

Ferries on Lake Balaton
During the summer season a ferry service operates at 40 minute intervals daily between Tihanyrév and Szántódrév from 6.20 a.m. to mindnight, in off season from 6.30 a.m. to 7.30 p.m.

Information on boat services

In Budapest
MAHART Passenger Boat Service, Budapest, V., Belgrád rakpart; Phone: 118-1704, telex: 22-5412.
MAHART Vigadó tér Boat Station; Phone: 118-1223
BKV Boat Station, Budapest, XIII., Jászai Mari tér.
Phone: 129-5844
On Lake Balaton
MAHART Balaton Branch Office, 8600 Siófok, Boat Station.
Phone: 84/10-050, telex: 22-5805.

By bus
All villages with at least 200 inhabitants can be reached by bus. There are also bus services from the bigger towns to resorts, excursion spots and spas. For departures and arrivals, contact the VOLÁN offices.

Information, ticket sales
Engels Square Bus Terminal, Budapest, V., Engels tér;
Phone: 118-2122
Domestic travel; Phone: 117-2966
Foreign services; Phone: 117-2562

By car
TRAFFIC REGULATIONS
Traffic regulations in Hungary are generally the same as in other European countries, but the following differences should be noted:
Speed limit:

in residential areas:	60 km/h
on main roads:	80 km/h
on highways:	100 km/h
on motorways:	120 km/h

Any changes in the speed limit are indicated by signs.
– Three-point safety belts must be fitted in the front seats.
– Children under six may not use the front seats.
– Use of the horn is forbidden in residential areas unless there is danger of accident.
– Dimmed headlights must be used from dusk to dawn and in conditions of poor visibility in villages, urban areas and on main roads.
– In Hungary there is a total ban on alcohol in the blood while driving.
– The use of auxiliary stop lights and of dark curtains of foils in the windows is forbidden.
– Motorcyclists and pillion passengers must wear crash helmets. The use of dimmed headlight is compulsory night and day. In case of an accident the police must be called immediately. Phone: 07. Damaged vehicles may leave the country only with the permission of the police.

INSURANCE CLAIMS
Claims must be made within 48 hours of an accident, and no later than the following working day.
In Budapest
HUNGARIA International Vehicle Insurance Office, Budapest, XIV., Gvadányi u. 69, 5th fl; Phone: 183-5350, 183-5359

In the country:
at country vehicle insurance branch offices.
Please note: Diesel oil can be purchased at petrol stations only for coupons. Coupons are available at IBUSZ offices, at border crossing stations and in hotels. It is advisable to calculate the required quantity of diesel oil in advance, as coupons are nonrefundable.

Information on road conditions:
UTINFORM
Phone: 122-2238, 122-7052

Car services
There are approx. 60 car services in Budapest and in the major towns. For adresses, opening hours and a list of services contact TOURINFORM, 117-9800

BREAKDOWN SERVICE '
1. *Hungarian Automobile Club* (MAK)
In case of a breakdown call the "yellow angels" of the breakdown service.
In Budapest:
— XIV., Francia út 38/a; Phone: 169-1831, 169-3714 (night and day), telex: 22-4210.
There are technical stations in major country towns.
Emergency telephones along the motorways:
— on the M7 Motorway at every second km between 6 and 108 kms, 8 a.m. to 6 p.m.
— on the M1 Motorway at the 36, 63 and 83 km posts
— on the M3 Motorway at the 27, 51 and 75 km posts
In the Danube Bend:
2000 Szentendre, Belső körút; Phone: 26/11-999
If the car cannot be repaired on the spot, the Automobile Club will tow it to the service station you indicate, or will arrange for the transport of the car abroad. Members of foreign automobile and touring clubs can pay for the expenses of the transport and repair by letter of credit.
2. *VOLÁN* (night and day)
Budapest, XV., Ifjúgárda utca 117; Phone: 140-9326
3. *FŐSPED*
Budapest, X., Kőér utca 3; Phone: 147-5594, 157-2811 (night and day).

RENT-A-CAR SERVICE
You can rent a car for Hungary anywhere in the world from Avis, Hertz, Europcar and Budget, and in Europe, also from Inter-Rent.
Representations and agencies in Hungary
FŐTAXI-HERTZ, Budapest, VII., Kertész utca 24;
Phone: 111-6116. At the airport: 157-9123
IBUSZ-AVIS, Budapest, V., Martinelli tér 8; Phone: 118-6222
At the airport: 147-5754
VOLÁNTOURIST-EUROPCAR, Budapest, IX., Vaskapu utca 16.
Phone: 133-4783
At the airport: Terminal 1; Phone: 134-2540, Terminal 2; Phone: 157-8519
COOPTOURIST-BUDGET, Budapest, IX., Ferenc körút 43; Phone: 113-1466. At the airport: 147-7328

Citizens of Western countries can rent cars only for foreign currency. Credit cards (Amex, Baymex, Visa, Eurocard, Mastercard) and travellers' cheques are accepted.
Conditions for car renting: The driver should be over 21, and should possess a driving licence for at least 1 year. The rental fee includes the compulsory third party insurance and maintenance fees.

USEFUL INFORMATION

Medical care
First aid and transport to hospitals are free for foreigners, while a charge is made for medical examination and treatment. Consulting rooms can ben found in all districts of the capital and in country towns, thus in bigger towns of the Balaton region. Foreigners are always accepted at the emergency rooms of hospitals and consulting rooms in villages.
Dental emergency service in Budapest
Institute of Stomatology, Budapest VIII., 40 Szentkirályi u.
Phone: 133-0970
Pharmacies can be found in all parts of the capital and in every village.

Ambulance:
call 04 day or night.

Lost property
For information on property lost on public transport vehicles contact the BKV office at Budapest, VII., 18 Akácfa u.; Phone: 122-6613.

Postal services
Post offices open seven days a week (night and day):
Budapest, VI., 105 Lenin körút (Western Railway Station)
Budapest, VIII., 11/c Baross tér (Eastern Railway Station).

Telex:
In addition to the hotel telex services there are four public telexes in Hungary:
— Budapest, V., 17/19 Petőfi Sándor utca
— Debrecen, Post Office No. 15, 18 Hajdú utca
— Keszthely, 1/3 Kossuth Lajos utca
— Miskolc, Post Office No. 4, 3/9 Széchenyi István utca

Photography
Photographic equipment and accessories are sold in OFO-TÉRT shops throughout the country. Some major shops in Budapest:
— V., 14 Tanács körút

- V., 2 Váci utca
- VII., 80 Rákóczi út

Quick photo service
in the FOTEX (American-Hungarian Photo Service) shops:
- Skála Metro Department Store, V., 1–3 Marx tér
- Skála Budapest Department Store, XI., 6–10 Schönherz Zoltán út, night and day
- VII., 2 Rákóczi út
- V., 9 Váci utca
FŐFOTO, 20 Szent István krt.
and the above OFOTÉRT shops.
Camera repairs: Budapest VII., 59 Akácfa utca

Public holidays

New Years Day	1 January
National Day	15 March
Easter Monday	
International Labour Day	1 May
Constitution Day	20 August
Day of the Republic	23 October
Christmas	25–26 December

Foreign-language radio broadcasts

The news is broadcasted daily on the Petőfi station in English, German and Russian starting at noon.
Danubius Radio: Tourism and commercial programmes broadcast in German by Hungarian Radio from 15 April to 31 October daily from 6.30 a.m. 10 p.m. on 100.5 MHz for Balaton and Western Hungary, and on 103.3 MHz for Budapest and Central Hungary. The programmes include travel information, music, international news and search services. Phone: 138-7840.
Esperanto News: on Sundays at 1.05 p.m. on the Bartók station. A ten-minute programme with tourist information, news, reports and current Esperanto topics.

Where to shop

Hotel shops, Konsumtourist and Utastourist shops sell goods for foreign currencies. Credit cards are also accepted.
UTASTOURIST
Balatonfüred, 9 Blaha Lujza utca
Balatonfüred, Railway Station
Balatonföldvár, Hotel Fesztivál
Tapolca, 4 Lenin tér
Pápa, 3 Fő út

Works of art

Paintings, works of art, Herend china, silverware, objects of folk art anc coins can be bought for convertible currency in the Konsumtourist shops of the Commission Company (BÁV) in Budapest and in the country. Your receipt serves as an export permit.
Budapest I., 3 Hess András tér; Phone: 175-0392
Budapest VI., 27 Népköztársaság útja; Phone: 142-5525
Szentendre, 13 Vöröshadsereg utca; Phone: 26/10-690
Szombathely, Mártírok tere 10
Sopron, 5 Színház utca; Phone: 99/12-731
Nagykanizsa, 8 Lenin utca
Wholesalers'shops:
Works of art and furniture:
KONSUMEX Foreign Trade Company
Budapest XIV., 162 Hungária körút; Phone:122-2655,
Telex: 22-5151
Paintings:
ARTEX Foreign Trade Company
Budapest V., 31 Münnich Ferenc utca; Phone: 153-0222,
Telex: 22-4951
Auctions are held in March during the Spring Festival and in July–August. For information contact:
Central BÁV (Commission) shop, Budapest IX., 12 Kinizsi utca; Phone: 117-6511
BÁV shop, Budapest V., 1–3 Bécsi utca; Phone: 117-2548
Shops selling art and antiques for Forints:
Budapest V., 1–3 Bécsi utca; Phone: 117-2548
Budapest V., 1–3 Kossuth L. utca; Phone: 117-3718
Budapest V., 3 Szent István körút; Phone: 131-4534
Budapest V., 3 Felszabadulás tér; Phone: 118-3381

Businessmen, Attention!

Placing your functioning capital
Joint venture regulations offer tax preference in certain areas of business. In the area of tourism, this involves three subjects:
- development of thermal and medicinal tourism in specified areas;
- renovation and utilization of protected historical mansions;
- development of hotel capacity in the capital and preferred resorts, especially in the moderate price category.
In these cases, profits of the joint venture are tax exempt for the first five years, while after the first five years of operation, the joint venture tax is only 20% instead of the usual 40%. If a previously defined part of your profits are reinvested in the venture, you will receive further tax cuts. Transfer of your hard currency home is guaranteed by the Transfer Guarantee of the National Bank of Hungary.
New regulations also make it possible for small private investors to become members of limited liability companies. Conditions: at least one Hungarian company partner, basic

capital investment of a least 100,000 Forints per founding member, and a minimum of 500,000 Forints of basic starter investment.

Organization and investments of joint ventures are handled by the International Agency for Capital Investment (1014 Budapest, 4 Babits Mihály köz). For further information contact Attila Csiki at the Ministry of Finance (Phone: 118-3663) or the head of the Joint Venture Club of the Chamber of Commerce, Iván Toldy Ősz (Phone: 153-3333).

Economic companies with foreign participation can get and treely use the right of ownership of the real estate needed to their activities.

Renting real estate

Apartments or summer houses may be rented for up to 30 years. The use of such real estate may be extended to close relatives. Rental rights may also be passed on to private people with staying permits; they may also inherit such rights. When the contract expires, the former tenant is given preferred treatment if he wishes to renew.

Opening an account

Foreign citizens may open foreign currency accounts at several Hungarian banks such as the National Savings Bank (OTP) and others. Interest is tax exempt and all accounts are secret, and the banks will not provide any information whatsoever about them. Interest rates fluctuate according to changes in the international money market, and many from the accounts may be transferred anywhere.

The HUNGARIAN FOREIGN TRADE BANK, LTD. is one of the main commercial banks of Hungary. Clients receive the best attention in financing foreign exchange and domestic Forint transactions, in opening and handling of foreign currency accounts. The best and most competitve conditions are guaranteed.

Offices in Budapest and elsewhere:

Budapest V., 11 Szent István tér
　　　　　Phone: (36-1) 132-9360 or 112-7830
　　　　　Telex: (61) 226941
　　　　　Telefax: (36-1) 132-2568
　　　　　SWIFT: MKKB HU HB
Győr　　 9021 Pf. 444 or 9002, 19 Bajcsy-Zsilinszky út
　　　　　Phone:06-96-18818, 06-96-15287 or 06-96-18711
　　　　　Telex: 24617
Pécs　　 7621, 3 Rákóczi út
　　　　　Phone: 06-72-32252 or 06-72-12277
　　　　　Telex: 12780
Szeged　 6724, 3–5 Eszperantó utca
　　　　　Phone: 06-62-14377
Szolnok　5002 Pf. 32 or 5000, 18 Kossuth Lajos utca
　　　　　Phone: 06-56-11238 or 06-56-13215
Business hours: Monday–Friday 8 a.m. to 3 p.m.
Cashier:　　　　Monday–Friday 9 a.m. to 1 p.m.

TOURIST INFORMATION

Published by Forma-Art
Publisher: István Sziklai
Managing editor: Rózsa Szalontay © 1990
Text: István Lázár

Translation: Zsuzsa Béres
Consultant: George Pándi

Captions, Sights to see: Gabriella Szvoboda–Dománszky,
Györgyi P. Simon

Typography: Vera Köböl

Editor staff: Sándor T. Antal, József Bessenyei, Éva
Moskovszky, Ágnes Padányi, Györgyi P. Simon, Rózsa
Szalontay, Gabriella Szvoboda–Dománszky, Tamás
Vízkelety

Fotos:
Lóránt Bérczy: 4
Imre Gál: 72, 95, 107
János Eifert: 115, 141, 154
Lajos Gál: 70, 139, 140
Károly Hemző: 11, 18, 26, 28, 47, 49, 60, 62, 73, 74, 133
Antal Kiss: 10, 17, 23, 75, 123, 136
Károly Kastaly: 71
Kornél Kovács – József Varga: 55, 56, 57, 58, 59
Lajos Köteles: 92, 117
József Pálmai: 1, 2
Miklós Sehr: 19, 77, 78, 106
Dr. József Szabó: 40, 68, 88, 111, 118, 126
Károly Szelényi: 6, 7, 9, 20, 22, 29, 30, 31, 32, 34, 36, 37, 38,
39, 48, 51, 52, 53, 54, 69, 76, 87, 90, 103, 104, 105, 119, 121,
125, 131, 132, 138, 142, 144, 145, 146, 147, 149
Ferenc Tulok: 93, 114, 129
IPV Archives: 8, 24, 25, 35, 41, 61, 65, 66, 67, 85, 86, 100, 113,
116, 124, 148, 151, 152, 153
KAK Archives: 3, 5, 16, 21, 33, 42, 43, 44, 45, 46, 50, 84, 91, 101,
102, 108, 109, 110, 112, 122, 127, 128, 130, 137, 143
MTI: 63, 79, 80, 81, 82, 83, 94, 96, 97, 98, 99, 150 and the back
cover

Cover: Dr. József Szabó
Front page: Károly Szelényi

ISBN 963 02 8031 0

Offset and Playing Cards Printing Office, Budapest
Manager: László Burger